The Best Yes

STUDY GUIDE

Also by Lysa TerKeurst

Am I Messing Up My Kids?

Becoming More Than a Good Bible Study Girl

Becoming More Than a Good Bible Study Girl video curriculum

The Best Yes

Capture His Heart (for wives)

Capture His Heart (for husbands)

Leading Women to the Heart of God

Living Life on Purpose

Made to Crave

Made to Crave Devotional

Made to Crave for Teens

Made to Crave video curriculum

Made to Crave Action Plan video curriculum

Unglued

Unglued Devotional

Unglued video curriculum

What Happens When Women Say Yes to God

What Happens When Women Say Yes to God video curriculum

What Happens When Women Walk in Faith

Who Holds the Key to Your Heart?

The Best Yes

MAKING WISE DECISIONS IN THE
MIDST OF ENDLESS DEMANDS

STUDY GUIDE
Six Sessions

LYSA TERKEURST

with Christine M. Anderson

NELSON
BOOKS
An Imprint of Thomas Nelson

Published in Nashville, Tennessee, by Nelson Books, an imprint of Thomas Nelson. Nelson Books and Thomas Nelson are registered trademarks of HarperCollins Christian Publishing, Inc.

Published in association with the literary agency of Fedd & Company, Inc., Post Office Box 341973, Austin, TX 78734.

Thomas Nelson titles may be purchased in bulk for educational, business, fund-raising, or sales promotional use. For information, please e-mail SpecialMarkets@ThomasNelson.com.

Scripture quotations marked NIV are taken from The Holy Bible, *New International Version*®, NIV®. Copyright © 1973, 1978, 1984, 2011 by Biblica, Inc.® Used by permission. All rights reserved worldwide. Quotations marked CEV are taken from the *Contemporary English Version*. Copyright © 1995 by American Bible Society. Used by permission. Quotations marked KJV are taken from the King James Version of the Bible. Quotations marked MSG are taken from *The Message*. Copyright © 1993, 1994, 1995, 1996, 2000, 2001, 2002. Used by permission of NavPress Publishing Group. Quotations marked NASB are taken from the *New American Standard Bible*. Copyright © 1960, 1962, 1963, 1968, 1971, 1972, 1973, 1975, 1977, 1995 by The Lockman Foundation. Used by permission. Quotations marked NKJV are taken from the New King James Version. Copyright © 1982 by Thomas Nelson, Inc. Used by permission. All rights reserved. Quotations marked NLT are taken from the *Holy Bible, New Living Translation*, copyright © 1996, 2004. Used by permission of Tyndale House Publishers, Inc., Wheaton, Illinois. All rights reserved. Quotations marked The Voice are taken from *The Voice Bible*, copyright © Thomas Nelson, Inc. *The Voice*™ translation, copyright © Ecclesia Bible Society. All rights reserved.

Page 32 photos: Popperfoto/Getty Images (top)
AFP/Getty Images (bottom)

ISBN 978-1-40020-596-7

First Printing June 2014/Printed in the United States of America

Contents

How to Use This Guide

GROUP SIZE

The Best Yes video study is designed to be experienced in a group setting such as a Bible study, Sunday school class, or any small group gathering. To ensure everyone has enough time to participate in discussions, it is recommended that large groups break up into smaller groups of four to six people each.

MATERIALS NEEDED

In addition to bringing a Bible to group discussions, each participant should have her own study guide, which includes notes for video segments, directions for activities and discussion questions, as well as personal studies to deepen learning between sessions. Each group should also have one copy of *The Best Yes* video for group viewing. We also recommend that each participant have a copy of *The Best Yes* book and read the corresponding chapters before coming together as a group. However, if your group would rather read the book chapters after meeting together, feel free to make that switch. Either way, reading the book is a great investment of your time.

FORMAT

The Best Yes study includes video-based group discussions, personal studies, and suggested reading in *The Best Yes* book. Here is a recommendation for how to make the most of the study components:

- Prior to each group session, read the suggested chapters in *The Best Yes* book. (Note that this is recommended but not required in order to participate in group discussions.)
- Attend the meeting, watch the video together, and process the video teaching using the group discussion questions.
- Between group sessions, complete the personal study (and read the suggested chapters in *The Best Yes* book if you haven't already done so).

TIMING

Groups that meet for differing lengths of time can use *The Best Yes* study. Each group session is timed for one hour but includes optional suggested times and discussions that expand the material to meet the needs of groups that meet for two hours or anywhere between one and two hours. Simply adjust the suggested times to fit your needs.

The time notations — for example (20 minutes) — indicate the *actual* time of video segments and the *suggested* times for each activity or discussion. Alternate time notations and optional activities for two-hour groups are set off with a gray background. For example:

The Fear of Decisions (10 minutes)

If your group meets for two hours, allow 20 minutes for this discussion.

In this example, one-hour groups allow 10 minutes for the discussion and two-hour groups allow 20 minutes for the discussion.

Adhering to the suggested times will enable you to complete each session in one or two hours. If your group meets for one hour, you may also opt to devote two meetings rather than one to each session. In addition to allowing discussions to be more spacious, this has the added advantage of allowing group members to complete the personal study between meetings. In the second meeting, devote the time allotted for watching the video to discussing group members' insights and questions from their reading and personal study.

FACILITATION

Each group should appoint a facilitator who is responsible for starting the video and for keeping track of time during discussions and activities. Facilitators may also read questions aloud and monitor discussions, prompting participants to respond and ensuring that everyone has the opportunity to participate.

PERSONAL STUDIES

Maximize the impact of the curriculum with additional study between group sessions. There are three personal study options for *The Best Yes* — thirty-minute, fifteen-minute, and five-minute. Go for the one that works best with your schedule that particular week; or, if you'd like, do all three.

Set Your Heart to Wisdom

The fear of the LORD is the beginning of wisdom.
Psalm 111:10 NIV

Recommended reading prior to the meeting:
The Best Yes book, chapters 1 – 3

WELCOME!

Welcome to Session 1 of *The Best Yes*. If this is your first time together as a group, take a moment to introduce yourselves to each other before watching the video. Then let's get started!

**OPTIONAL DISCUSSION:
SAY YES, SAY NO (15 MINUTES)**

Use this discussion if time permits or if your group meets for two hours.

❧

The Best Yes study is about how to use two powerful words — yes and no — to make wise decisions. But yes and no are also great words you can use to get to know each other better. Go around the group and respond to as many of the following questions as you have time for. See how much you can find out about each other simply by answering yes or no.

- Do you like spicy food?
- Have you ever Googled yourself?
- Did you laugh out loud today?
- Have you ever broken a bone?
- Do you like your signature?
- Have you ever cried to avoid getting a speeding ticket?
- Have you ever had your name in a newspaper or other publication?
- Do you still have your tonsils?
- Have you ever secretly skipped pages when reading a bedtime story?

- Can you say the alphabet backward?
- Have you ever fallen asleep at work?
- Do you cry at weddings?
- Did yesterday turn out like you thought it would?
- Do you like to spend time by yourself?

VIDEO:
Set Your Heart to Wisdom (15 minutes)

Play the video segment for Session 1. As you watch, use the outline provided to follow along or to take additional notes on anything that stands out to you.

Notes

A heart must have godly wisdom or it will follow the pattern of foolishness.

"The fear of the LORD is the beginning of wisdom" (Psalm 111:10 NIV).

Head knowledge of the fear of the Lord:

- **Fear:** There are two Hebrew words for "fear" in the Bible. One is *pachad* (pakh'-ad), which means terror. That's not the word used in this verse. The word used is *yir'ah* (yir-aw'), which means a reverence for God.

  "The expression describes that reverential attitude or holy fear which man, when his heart is set aright, observes toward God" (*Matthew Henry Commentary*). To observe toward God is to look for the hand of God in everything.

When we have a reverential attitude and look for the hand of God in everything, we start seeing things from the perspective of wisdom. This becomes our focus.

* **Lord:** I need to anchor my heart to the Lord so I can set my heart to the wisdom of God.

    Jesus is "the power of God and the wisdom of God" (1 Corinthians 1:24 NIV).

    In Christ "are hidden all the treasures of wisdom and knowledge" (Colossians 2:3 NIV).

* Once Jesus is the Lord of our heart and the focus of our heart, we have unlocked the door to obtaining God's wisdom.

Heart knowledge of the fear of the Lord:

"My son, if you accept my words and store up my commands within you, turning your ear to wisdom and applying your heart to understanding — indeed, if you call out for insight and cry aloud for understanding, and if you look for it as for silver and search for it as for hidden treasure, then you will understand the fear of the LORD and find the knowledge of God. For the LORD gives wisdom; from his mouth come knowledge and understanding" (Proverbs 2:1 – 6 NIV).

* *Accept my words.* Get into God's Word.

* *Store up my commands.* Let God's Word get into you.

* *Turn your ear to wisdom.* Listen to wise instruction from God and wise people.

- *Apply your heart to understanding.* Apply wise instruction to your current situation.

- *Call out for insight.* Ask God for insights you wouldn't think of on your own.

- *Cry aloud.* Pray out loud over situations where you need wisdom.

- *Look for it.* Actively look for God's revelations. Look for the hand of God in everything.

- *Search for it as hidden treasure.* Treat wisdom as one of the greatest treasures you could acquire.

set up time

We have to choose to follow the Lord, not just with our salvation decision but also with our daily decisions.

Wisdom and folly both want to control our lives, and we have to make a choice about which one will.

you make decisions. The decisions make you!

This Week: Identify a situation in your life where you need to discern a Best Yes, and match it with a verse or several verses from Proverbs. Apply and pray those verses. Talk about them with your wise friends. Wisdom will be waiting for you.*

My Thoughts:

---

* See the Session 1 personal study "Ten Times Wise" for additional guidance in completing this assignment.

GROUP DISCUSSION:
Video Debrief (5 minutes)

1. What part of the teaching had the most impact on you?

The Fear of Decisions (10 minutes)

> If your group meets for two hours, allow 20 minutes
> for this discussion.

2. Which of the following statements would you say best describes your schedule right now?

   - ❑ *Time to spare.* I am mostly unscheduled and have quite a bit of discretionary time.
   - ❑ *Time accessible.* I am lightly scheduled and have a fair amount of discretionary time.
   - ❑ *Time enough.* I have a good balance between scheduled commitments and discretionary time.
   - ❑ *Time limited.* I am heavily scheduled and have little discretionary time.
   - ❑ *Time shortage.* I am overscheduled and very rarely have discretionary time.

   - ⚹ What three words would you use to summarize how you feel about your current schedule? For example: *challenged, bored, energized, exhausted, resentful, engaged, productive,* etc.

     Productive
     Bored

   - ⚹ How we schedule our time is based on the decisions we make — what we say yes or no to. Overall, how much control do you feel you have over your schedule right now? In other words, to what degree do you feel free to say yes or no to the requests and opportunities that come your way?

+ What factors, if any, tend to make you feel afraid or anxious about saying no?

The Fear of the Lord (10 minutes)

> If your group meets for two hours, allow 25 minutes for this discussion.

3. Left unchecked, even small fears can derail our decisions. Therefore, we need to flip the fear in our decision making into a much healthier fear that leads to wisdom:

> The fear of the LORD is the beginning of wisdom; all who follow his precepts have good understanding.
> (Psalm 111:10 NIV)

Go around the group and have a different person read aloud the following verses that describe various aspects of what it means to fear the Lord. As the verses are read, keep in mind that you are looking for connections between the fear of the Lord and wisdom. Underline any words or phrases that stand out to you. You may wish to read through the list twice to give everyone time to listen and respond.

> The LORD watches over those who fear him, those who rely on his unfailing love.
> (Psalm 33:18 NLT)

ॐ

Work hard to show the results of your salvation, obeying God
with deep reverence and fear. For God is working in you, giving you the desire and the power to do what pleases him.
(Philippians 2:12–13 NLT)

ॐ

But you [God] offer forgiveness, that we might learn
to fear you.
(Psalm 130:4 NLT)

ॐ

He grants the desires of those who fear him; he hears their
cries for help and rescues them.
(Psalm 145:19 NLT)

ॐ

X   Teach me your way, LORD, that I may rely on your faithfulness;
give me an undivided heart, that I may fear your name.
(Psalm 86:11 NIV)

ॐ

How joyful are those who fear the LORD — all who follow
his ways!
(Psalm 128:1 NLT)

✦ In order to fear the Lord in the way we're learning, we have to
know Him and understand what He's like. Briefly review the passages and focus on the words describing God's actions. Overall,
how does God relate to those who fear Him? What is the image
of God these passages convey?
caring God.

✦ The passages also characterize those who fear the Lord. What
stands out most to you about what it means to fear the Lord?
What connections might you make between these characteris-
tics and what it means to practice wisdom?
Grant
Desires   Obey
Joy   Relay on
Rescued.   faithful Love.
willing accepting

❖ If part of what it means to fear the Lord — to have wisdom — is to rely on God's unfailing love and faithfulness, what do you think it means to be foolish in this regard? In other words, what else might we choose to rely on instead (especially when making decisions)?

Own way   not follow his
Own Time   Comands
Turn our Backs

❖ When you feel anxious or afraid about saying yes or no, which passage(s) might help you to flip your fear of the decision into a healthier fear — the fear of the Lord that leads to wisdom? Share the reasons for your response.

The Best Yes (10 minutes)

> If your group meets for two hours, allow 20 minutes for this discussion.

4. It's easy to think that our daily yes and no decisions aren't all that important, but over time, they can add up: The decisions we make dictate the schedules we keep; the schedules we keep determine the life we live; the life we live determines how we spend our soul — and how we spend our soul matters.

    Briefly recall a recent decision you made about your time that you later realized was unwise.

    ❖ How did that decision impact your schedule?

+ How did your schedule then impact your life?

+ As a result, how would you say you spent your soul in that situation?

5. The promise of *The Best Yes* is that we can learn to move beyond the limitations of yes and no and seek out a third option: the Best Yes. A Best Yes decision is a choice that allows us to play our part in God's plan—to spend our energy, focus, and passion on the assignments that are really ours.

    + Sometimes we miss our Best Yes opportunities because we fail to heed the warning of the whispers within: *I'm tired. I don't want to say yes. I'm a little overwhelmed and a lot worn down.* Looking back on the situation you described in question 4, were there any warning whispers you failed to heed? If so, what were they?

    + What do you imagine a Best Yes decision in that situation might have been? In other words, what decision would have enabled you to play your part and spend your energy, focus, and passion wisely?

Becoming a Best Yes Group (8 minutes)

> If your group meets for two hours, allow 20 minutes
> for this discussion.

6. The five remaining sessions in *The Best Yes* explore how to establish a pattern of wisdom in our lives, especially in the decisions we make about how to use our time. In addition to learning together as a group, it's important to be aware of how God is at work among you in the time you spend together — especially in how you relate to each other and share your lives throughout the study. As you discuss the teaching in each session, there will be many opportunities to speak life-giving — and life-challenging — words, and to listen to one another deeply.

   Take a few moments to consider the kinds of things that are important to you in this setting. What do you need or want from the other members of the group? Use one or more of the sentence starters below, or your own statement, to help the group understand the best way to be good companions to you throughout this Best Yes journey. As each person responds, use the chart that follows to briefly note what is important to that person and how you can support and encourage her.

   It really helps me when . . .
   I tend to withdraw or feel anxious when . . .
   I'd like you to challenge me about . . .
   I'll know this group is a safe place if you . . .
   In our discussions, the best thing you could do for me is . . .

Name	The Best Way I Can Encourage and Help This Person Is . . .
Vicki	Safe place
Amy	Comfortable
Norma	Needs To feel ok not perfect -
Leslie	Needs a Calendar
Lois	Needs Someone To follow Time To make connect

Name	The Best Way I Can Encourage and Help This Person Is ...
Valerie	
Tammi	Prayer anxiety

INDIVIDUAL ACTIVITY:
What I Want to Remember (2 minutes)

Complete this activity on your own.

1. Briefly review the outline and any notes you took.
2. In the space below, write down the most significant thing you gained in this session — from the teaching, activities, or discussions.

What I want to remember from this session ...

CLOSING PRAYER

Close your time together with prayer. Share your prayer requests with one another. Ask God to give you the joy Scripture promises to those who learn to fear Him, and invite Him to lead you into the freedom of making wise, Best Yes decisions.

GO DEEPER WITH *THE BEST YES*

For additional teaching and insights, read the following chapters in *The Best Yes* book if you haven't already done so:

1. Check the Third Box
2. The Way of the Best Yes
3. Overwhelmed Schedule, Underwhelmed Soul

OPTIONAL GROUP CHALLENGE: WISE UP

<u>Wisdom</u> is the ability to cope with the demands of life in healthy and constructive ways. And the book of Proverbs is rich with practical guidance to help us apply biblical wisdom to the demands we face every day. You probably already know some popular proverbs, and perhaps you've even done a study on the book of Proverbs, but maybe you have yet to read it from beginning to end. If so, now is your chance!

The book of Proverbs is conveniently divided into thirty one chapters, the perfect amount to cover in about a month. By reading one chapter a day, six to seven days a week over the next five weeks, you can read through the entire book of Proverbs by the time your group gathers for the final session in *The Best Yes* study:

Week 1: Proverbs 1 – 7
Week 2: Proverbs 8 – 13
Week 3: Proverbs 14 – 19
Week 4: Proverbs 20 – 25
Week 5: Proverbs 26 – 31

The <u>challenge is optiona</u>l, so there's no guilt, no pressure, no have-tos! In fact, use this as an opportunity to practice making your first Best Yes decision. If you're up for the challenge and would enjoy it, great! (A reading worksheet is provided on the next page and in subsequent sessions to track your reading and insights.) If it's just one thing too many right now, your group will cheer you on when you honor your limits by saying, "I can't this time." There is no wrong answer — just a Best Yes invitation to make the wisest choice for yourself right now.

Wise Up

WEEK 1 READING WORKSHEET

If you're participating in the optional challenge to read through the book of Proverbs, use this worksheet to help you keep track of your reading. If you'd like, use the space provided below to make notes and to reflect on what you read this week.

❏ Proverbs 1   ❏ Proverbs 5

❏ Proverbs 2   ❏ Proverbs 6

❏ Proverbs 3   ❏ Proverbs 7

❏ Proverbs 4

What verses, words, or phrases stand out most to you? Why?

A Best Yes is you playing your part.

At church.

At school.

At work.

At wherever you are today.

And what's so great about that?

In God's plan, you've got a part to play.

If you know it and believe it, you'll live it.

You'll live your life making decisions

with the Best Yes as your best filter.

You'll be a grand display

of God's Word lived out.

INTRODUCTION:
Make Your Personal Studies a Best Yes

Every session in *The Best Yes* includes a personal study to help you make meaningful connections between your life and what you're learning each week. Because all of us sometimes have days and weeks that are more demanding than others, each personal study features three segments designed to fit whatever time you have:

+ 30-Minute Wisdom
+ 15-Minute Wisdom
+ 5-Minute Wisdom

Together, the time allotted for the three segments adds up to fifty minutes. If you'd like to spread it out, devoting about eight to ten minutes a day to the study will enable you to work through all three segments in the course of a week. If you have one day a week with a larger block of time, you might choose to work through all three segments in one sitting. Or, if all you can spare is fifteen minutes, completing the fifteen-minute segment could be the perfect solution for you that week. There's no right or wrong way to do the personal studies! You're free to make a Best Yes decision by customizing an option that best fits your needs and schedule from week to week.

Session 1

Personal Study

FINDING YOUR "SOUL THING"

> There's this nagging sense that something's a bit off inside me. Someone makes a request of me that I know right away is unrealistic. My brain says no. My schedule says no. My reality says no. But my heart says yes! Then my mouth betrays my intention of saying no, as it smiles and says, "Yes, of course."
>
> *The Best Yes*, page 4

1. Think back on a recent situation in which you said yes, even though at the time you knew that probably wasn't the wisest response. Write what you were thinking in the thought bubble below; then write what you actually said in the speech bubble.

Something happened that changed your "no" thoughts into a "yes" re-sponse. What was it? What concerns or fears prompted you to disregard the warnings from your discernment or the Holy Spirit's leading?

To what degree does your response in this particular situation represent your general decision-making approach when it comes to how you spend your time? Circle the number on the continuum that best describes your response.

1   2   3   4   5   6   7   8   9   10

My decision-making approach is reactive.
Other people's requests determine how I spend my time.

My decision-making approach is proactive.
My priorities determine how I spend my time.

2. A woman who lives with the stress of an overwhelmed schedule will often ache with the sadness of an underwhelmed soul. An underwhelmed soul is one who knows there is more God made her to do, but who feels too overwhelmed or powerless to pursue it.

    In what ways, if any, would you say your soul feels under-whelmed or lacking in fulfillment right now?

What is your "soul thing" — that God-honoring endeavor that keeps slipping away because there's been no time to set aside and actually start? What interests or dreams might you pursue, how-ever small or large, if you had the time and energy? For example: turn a photography hobby into a business, start a small bakery, go on a missions trip, get out of debt, go back and complete a degree, run a backyard Bible club for neighborhood kids, teach a class at church, etc.

If devoting time to this soul thing could be a Best Yes — a way for you to shine and serve in one of God's assignments for you — who might be blessed as a result? For example:

- ✤ *I want to turn my photography hobby into a business so that I might bless families with young children.*
- ✤ *I want to start a small bakery so that I might bless my family, my employees, and the customers I would serve each day.*
- ✤ *I want to go on a missions trip so that I might bless people who have fewer material resources than I do.*

I want to . . .

So that I might bless . . .

If I want things about my life to change, if I want to change the way I use the world's two most powerful words, *yes* and *no*, it won't happen just by trying harder or dreaming more or even working myself to death. I have to change my approach to the way I make decisions. The same patterns will produce the same habits. The same habits will lead to the same decisions. The same decisions will keep me stuck. And I don't want to be stuck.

The Best Yes, page 21

FEARLESS FOSBURY

I've got to become a Fearless Fosbury.

Now before you read any further, y'all know I'm not a sports girl.… But I found this story about an athlete who changed his approach and what a difference it made. He was a high jumper named Dick Fosbury.… With the traditional approach to the high jump, an athlete could only go so high. But Fosbury had the crazy idea of going higher by lowering his center of gravity. All he had to do was go headfirst and backward. That's why they call him Fearless. Using the new technique — which used to frighten his coaches — Fosbury set an Olympic record. Of course, he never could

Traditional feet-first jump

Fosbury's headfirst jump

have done that with the old technique. He had to change his approach if he wanted to improve his abilities. So he did just that.

He tried a new technique. He established new patterns. He changed his approach. And not only did he gain the highest level of success in doing all these things, he transformed the sport. Today,

more than forty years later, jumpers are still using the Fosbury technique. What if we, like Fosbury, decided to flip our current decision-making technique?…

It's not that how we've been living is bad — just like Fosbury's old jumping method wasn't a bad method. He still cleared the bar. But he dreamed of more, higher heights. And I suspect that's true for you too. Dick Fosbury discovered his new heights in being able to jump over his obstacle by turning his body so that his back went over before his feet.

That's an interesting concept to me.

He literally backed into his jump.

And when I think about the changes we need to make so our thing doesn't keep getting crowded out, I think we may have to back into it as well. Instead of waiting for the time to get started to simply appear one day, we need to be intentional with scheduling it.

The Best Yes, pages 19 – 20, 23

3. To get an inspiring picture of what can happen when we take a risk and change our approach, read the "Fearless Fosbury" story.

    When we get locked into a reactive approach to scheduling our time, chances are good that we'll spend our soul haphazardly. In order to spend our souls wisely and well, we need to flip our approach and be proactive — we must dedicate time to our soul thing each week before that time gets eaten up by other people's requests.

    Use the charts that follow to do a brief "hours assessment" of a typical week. For now, the goal is not to do a detailed analysis of your schedule but to get a quick snapshot of potential white space on your calendar. Rest assured, you're not committing to anything; you can come back later and make any necessary adjustments.

    Based on what you know about your schedule, block out an X for all the hours that are already occupied by nonnegotiables and commitments you value. Things you might consider include:

    - Sleep
    - Meals (prep, eating, cleanup)
    - Quiet time
    - Exercise
    - Family time
    - Work
    - Church (attending, serving, small group study)
    - Prep time for work or personal projects
    - Volunteer commitments
    - Date night
    - Kids' activities
    - Time with friends
    - Other priority events

    Once you've blocked out all the occupied hours, circle any white spaces that are left.

Example

Time	Sunday	Monday	Tuesday	Wednesday	Thursday	Friday	Saturday
6:00 p.m. ↓ 7:00 p.m.	X	X	X	X	X	X	X
7:00 p.m. ↓ 8:00 p.m.	O	O	X	X	O	X	X

Time	Sunday	Monday	Tuesday	Wednesday	Thursday	Friday	Saturday
6:00 a.m. ↓ 7:00 a.m.							
7:00 a.m. ↓ 8:00 a.m.							
8:00 a.m. ↓ 9:00 a.m.							
9:00 a.m. ↓ 10:00 a.m.							
10:00 a.m. ↓ 11:00 a.m.							
11:00 a.m. ↓ 12:00 p.m.							
12:00 p.m. ↓ 1:00 p.m.							
1:00 p.m. ↓ 2:00 p.m.							
2:00 p.m. ↓ 3:00 p.m.							
3:00 p.m. ↓ 4:00 p.m.							
4:00 p.m. ↓ 5:00 p.m.							
5:00 p.m. ↓ 6:00 p.m.							

Time	Sunday	Monday	Tuesday	Wednesday	Thursday	Friday	Saturday
6:00 p.m. ↓ 7:00 p.m.							
7:00 p.m. ↓ 8:00 p.m.							
8:00 p.m. ↓ 9:00 p.m.							
9:00 p.m. ↓ 10:00 p.m.							
10:00 p.m. ↓ 11:00 p.m.							
11:00 p.m. ↓ 12:00 a.m.							
12:00 a.m. ↓ 1:00 a.m.							
1:00 a.m. ↓ 2:00 a.m.							
2:00 a.m. ↓ 3:00 a.m.							
3:00 a.m. ↓ 4:00 a.m.							
4:00 a.m. ↓ 5:00 a.m.							
5:00 a.m. ↓ 6:00 a.m.							

If you feel ready to move ahead, choose one of the white spaces you circled and block it on your calendar as your "Best Yes" appointment. Even if you have no more than an hour, use this time to dream a little about what you would like to do. Write down your ideas and identify one next step. Before your time is done, look ahead on your calendar and schedule additional Best Yes time each week for the next few weeks. Every hour you dedicate to that Best Yes thing God made you to do, you spend your soul wisely and well.

4. Read Psalm 32:8 – 11, which describes God's promise to guide us with His love. Use the psalm as a reference for writing your own prayer. Name the decisions or challenges you face and ask the Lord to counsel you. Surrender your will and your desires to God's care. Receive His love and thank Him for leading you into wisdom.

Session 1

Personal Study

CHALKING UP WISDOM

The author of Proverbs offers clear instruction on how we can position ourselves for wisdom:

> My son, if you accept my words and store up my commands within you, turning your ear to wisdom and applying your heart to understanding — indeed, if you call out for insight and cry aloud for understanding, and if you look for it as for silver and search for it as for hidden treasure, then you will understand the fear of the LORD and find the knowledge of God. For the LORD gives wisdom; from his mouth come knowledge and understanding.
>
> (Proverbs 2:1 – 6 NIV)

The passage describes the acquisition of wisdom as a collaboration that requires both human intentionality and divine generosity. Our part in the process involves two kinds of initiative — we *take in* the wisdom we have, and then we *seek out* the wisdom we lack.

We *take in* the wisdom we have when we:

- Accept God's words
- Store up God's commands within us
- Turn our ears to wisdom
- Apply our heart to understanding

We *seek out* the wisdom we lack when we:

+ Call out for insight and cry aloud for understanding
+ Look for wisdom as for silver
+ Search for it as for hidden treasure

Use the questions on the two charts that follow to reflect on your heart — where you are *right now* — and what steps you might take to move forward — to take wisdom in and seek it out.

	Instructions from Proverbs	Where I Am Right Now	What I Need to Do to Move Forward
TAKE IN WISDOM	**Accept God's words.** Receiving wisdom begins with the posture of your heart toward God and Scripture—you must be willing to accept the Bible's teachings not just as generally authoritative, but also as valid and true for *you*.	How would you describe the posture of your heart right now? To what degree are you surrendered to God and the authority of Scripture?	
	Store up God's commands within you. This requires continually reflecting on biblical truths and committing them to memory so you are prepared when wisdom is needed.	To what degree are you willing or resistant to immersing yourself in Scripture and memorizing biblical truths? How prepared do you feel to draw on stored-up wisdom should it be needed?	
	Turn your ears to wisdom. Turning your ears toward wisdom requires turning them away from competing and conflicting voices.	What voices—internal or external—might be competing or conflicting with your ability to hear and receive wisdom?	
	Apply your heart to understanding. To apply the heart to understanding is to move beyond merely listening and paying attention; it requires desiring or loving what is heard and embracing it.	What is the posture of your heart in this regard? Are you tilted more toward reluctance or love when it comes to biblical wisdom?	

Instructions from Proverbs	Where I Am Right Now	What I Need in Order to Move Forward
Call out for insight and cry aloud for understanding. Take initiative and acknowledge your need for wisdom. Invite a wise friend, mentor, or pastor to listen to you and provide guidance. Or take it up a notch — raise your voice and persevere in a greater effort.	Have you asked God for help and insight through prayer? Remember, there's a difference between thinking about something and praying about it. Who is a trustworthy source of godly wisdom you can seek out for help?	
Look for it as for silver. Consider your approach to financial and material resources — specifically, the way you think about acquiring more of what you want and the care and attention you give to managing what you have.	What would it look like to devote the same level of mental energy and care to acquiring more wisdom?	
Search for it as for hidden treasure. A treasure is something that is exceedingly precious and valuable. The only reasonable response to a hidden treasure is to do whatever it takes to obtain it (Matthew 13:44).	What sacrifices — of time, resources, or lesser loves — might you have to make in order to acquire the wisdom you seek? What might have to change within you so you could make such sacrifices joyfully?	

SEEK OUT WISDOM

Briefly review the responses on your two charts. How do you sense God may be inviting you to move forward in taking wisdom in and seeking it out in one specific situation you are facing right now?

I can take in wisdom by …

I can seek out wisdom by …

Read Proverbs 2:9 – 11, which describes the promised benefits of positioning yourself for wisdom. Offer any insights from your charts to God, asking Him for what you need in order to take your next steps in pursuing wisdom.

Session 1

Personal Study

TEN TIMES WISE

One of the ways we can turn our ears to wisdom and apply our heart to understanding (Proverbs 2:2) is to make a direct match between the wisdom of Proverbs and the challenges we face. Even if you aren't able to participate in the optional group challenge to read through the entire book of Proverbs, you can still access the best of the wisdom it has to offer by spending just a few minutes each week with this recurring segment, "Ten Times Wise." Throughout the study, "Ten Times Wise" gathers up ten diverse and practical wisdom nuggets from Proverbs for you to reflect on and apply to your daily challenges and decisions. If you're short on time, "Ten Times Wise" is a one-stop shop for bite-size wisdom you can rely on every day.

Briefly identify a situation for which you need wisdom to discern a Best Yes in the near future.

Read through the ten verses from Proverbs on the following page. Check the box next to any verse that might relate to your issue. Now consider how the verse or verses you checked might apply to your situation and write down any connections you recognize.

Make the verse or verses you checked the focus of your prayer. Ask God to help you apply this wisdom as you seek to make a Best Yes choice.

TEN PROVERBS

❑ Better to be patient than powerful; better to have self-control than to conquer a city (Proverbs 16:32 NLT).

❑ Do away with any talk that twists and distorts the truth; have nothing to do with any verbal trickery (Proverbs 4:24 The Voice).

❑ By pride comes nothing but strife, but with the well-advised is wisdom (Proverbs 13:10 NKJV).

❑ Whoever puts down another is not wise, but one who knows better keeps quiet (Proverbs 11:12 The Voice).

❑ When you're kind to others, you help yourself; when you're cruel to others, you hurt yourself (Proverbs 11:17 MSG).

❑ A gossip betrays a confidence, but a trustworthy person keeps a secret (Proverbs 11:13 NIV).

❑ The generous will prosper; those who refresh others will themselves be refreshed (Proverbs 11:25 NLT).

❑ Fools have short fuses and explode all too quickly; the prudent quietly shrug off insults (Proverbs 12:16 MSG).

❑ Let the wise listen and add to their learning, and let the discerning get guidance (Proverbs 1:5 NIV).

❑ The fear of the Lord is the beginning of knowledge, but fools despise wisdom and instruction (Proverbs 1:7 NIV).

Establish a Pattern of Wisdom

A wise woman called from the city, "Listen! Listen!"
2 Samuel 20:16 NIV

Recommended reading prior to the meeting:
The Best Yes book, chapters 4 – 6

GROUP DISCUSSION:
Checking In (5 minutes)

> If your group meets for two hours, allow 15 minutes
> for this discussion.

A key part of getting to know God better is sharing your journey with others. Before watching the video, briefly check in with each other about your experiences since the last session. For example:

+ What insights did you discover in the personal study, reading through Proverbs, or in the chapters you read from *The Best Yes* book?
+ How did the last session impact your daily life or your relationship with God?
+ What questions would you like to ask the other members of your group?

VIDEO:
Establish a Pattern of Wisdom (18 minutes)

Play the video segment for Session 2. As you watch, use the outline provided to follow along or to take additional notes on anything that stands out to you.

Notes

The story of one wise woman (2 Samuel 20).

The larger context for the story is that David had recently learned a valuable lesson about dealing with troublemakers like his son Absalom.

David knew that Sheba the troublemaker had to be taken care of.

Joab, the commander of David's army, goes to find Sheba.

In the midst of her everyday life, the wise woman of Abel Beth Maakah calls down to Joab the commander.

Three lessons we can learn from this one wise woman:

1. *Approach*
   She had great courage.

   She was servant-hearted.

   God sees, God notices, God cares. He gives us gifts of wisdom with each of our gifts of service. God develops our character to match our calling.

   "With humility comes wisdom" (Proverbs 11:2 NIV).

2. *Assurance*
   She stood in the reality of truth rather than the reality of her circumstances.

   Her assurance came from the truth.

3. *Advice*
   When she went to people with her wise advice, they immediately listened to her because she had already established a pattern of wisdom in her life.

A wise woman makes wise decisions today that are still good for tomorrow.

This Week: Practice making wise decisions.

- *Be servant-hearted.* Do something for another person without grumbling. Trust that God sees, God knows, and through this act of service, God will develop your character to match your calling.
- *Stand in assurance.* Trump your feelings with truth. Just because you *feel* incapable/offended/insecure doesn't mean you need to *be* incapable/offended/insecure.
- *Tuck wisdom into your life.* Practice it in the things you say and in the things you choose not to say.

My Thoughts:

GROUP DISCUSSION:
Video Debrief (5 minutes)

If your group meets for two hours, allow 10 minutes for this discussion.

1. What part of the teaching had the most impact on you?

The Wise Woman and Joab (15 minutes)

> If your group meets for two hours, allow 35 minutes
> for this discussion.

2. In the encounter between Joab and the woman of Abel Beth Maakah, Scripture makes it very clear that she is a woman whose life is marked by wisdom. What is perhaps less obvious is how Joab stands in stark contrast to her as a man whose life is marked by foolishness. To get a clearer picture of Joab, go around the group and have a different person read aloud each of the facts about him listed in the following sidebar. Use these facts as a reference for your discussion.

   ♦ What words would you use to describe Joab? Consider such things as his temperament, ambitions, insecurities, etc.

   Does what he wants
   Does not follow rules.

   ♦ How would you characterize Joab's mental and emotional state as he approached Abel Beth Maakah in pursuit of Sheba?

   ♦ How do these facts about Joab influence your understanding of what the wise woman was up against when she asked to meet with Joab?
   She had the strength from God.

SEVEN FACTS ABOUT JOAB

In the early years of David's rise to power as king of Israel, Joab repeatedly demonstrated great bravery and success in battle and was fiercely loyal to David. However, as time went on, Joab's ambitions, insecurities, and misapplied loyalty led him to make some rash and foolish choices.

- While he was captain of David's army, Joab defied David's peace treaty and murdered Abner to avenge the death of Joab's brother, whom Abner had killed in self-defense (2 Samuel 3:21 – 27, 30).
- When David discovered Joab had killed Abner, he pronounced a curse on Joab and his family (2 Samuel 3:28 – 29); led a dramatic public mourning ritual and burial for Abner (2 Samuel 3:31 – 36); denounced Joab and his deeds as evil; and acknowledged that, although he was king, he was too weak to control Joab (2 Samuel 3:38 – 39).
- Convinced that he knew better, Joab disregarded David's orders to, "Protect the young man Absalom for my sake," and killed Absalom (2 Samuel 18:9 – 15).
- As he prepared to deal with Sheba's rebellion, David displaced Joab twice. He first appointed a commander named Amasa, and then put Joab's brother, Abishai, in charge of Joab's men (2 Samuel 20:4 – 7).
- Joab did not respond well to being displaced. He murdered Amasa, took control of Amasa's men, and took back his command from Abishai (2 Samuel 20:8 – 13). He then went after the rebel Sheba.

- After locating Sheba at Abel Beth Maakah, Joab's first action was to lay siege to the city (2 Samuel 20:14 – 15). It was an Israelite city, which he had no authority to attack. He made no offer of peace before attacking, which God had commanded Israel to do when going to war with its enemies (Deuteronomy 20:10 – 12). And the city he attacked was not just any city but one known for preserving God's law and maintaining stability in the region (2 Samuel 20:18 – 19). Tensions were already high, and Joab's siege had the potential to escalate from Sheba's rebellion into all-out civil war.
- Many years later while on his deathbed, David urged his son Solomon to bring Joab to justice for the murders of Abner and Amasa; Solomon summarily had Joab killed (1 Kings 2:5 – 6, 29 – 34).

3. Just as the woman of Abel calls out to Joab, the book of Proverbs often portrays the virtue of wisdom as a woman who constantly calls out to those who are foolish, generously offering knowledge and insight to any who will listen (Proverbs 1:20 – 23; 8:1 – 6; 9:1 – 6). As you read the following interaction between the wise woman and Joab, look for the ways the woman's words and actions portray wisdom, and how Joab's words demonstrate what it means to turn from foolishness and heed wisdom's call.

> While they were battering the wall to bring it down, a wise woman called from the city, "Listen! Listen! Tell Joab to come here so I can speak to him." He went toward her, and she asked, "Are you Joab?"
>
> "I am," he answered.
>
> She said, "Listen to what your servant has to say."

She was able to focus to ~

"I'm listening," he said.

She continued, "Long ago they used to say, 'Get your answer at Abel,' and that settled it. We are the peaceful and faithful in Israel. You are trying to destroy a city that is a mother in Israel. Why do you want to swallow up the LORD's inheritance?"

"Far be it from me!" Joab replied, "Far be it from me to swallow up or destroy! That is not the case. A man named Sheba son of Bikri, from the hill country of Ephraim, has lifted up his hand against the king, against David. Hand over this one man, and I'll withdraw from the city."

The woman said to Joab, "His head will be thrown to you from the wall."

(2 Samuel 20:15 – 21 NIV)

We all have a little bit of the one wise woman and a little bit of Joab within us.

+ What patterns do you see in Joab's life?

• Impulsive

+ What patterns do you see in the one wise woman's life?

N   Calm
Focused
assertive Resp. way

+ How do you see these patterns in your own life?

all these.

+ How can you take this instruction and make wiser patterns in your life?

Listen
wait
Patient

Key Lessons from One Wise Woman (15 minutes)

If your group meets for two hours, allow 25 minutes
for this discussion.

4. ***First Lesson: She was wise in her approach.*** Despite the fact that
   she was being attacked, the wise woman adopted a servant-hearted
   approach.

   ✤ We expect the wise woman to serve her city well, and she does.
     But she also humbly puts herself in service to Joab, her attacker.
     In what ways does the wise woman serve Joab well?

   She caused him to refocus.
   No power struggle

   ✤ Overall, would you say the wise woman's demeanor and the way
     she serves Joab challenges or reinforces your ideas about what
     it means to be humble and servant-hearted? Share the reasons
     for your response.

   yes - since God was in control

   ✤ When you think of what it means for you to be humble and
     servant-hearted, especially in the midst of everyday tasks
     and stresses, what do you find most challenging or encourag-
     ing about the wise woman's approach?

5. ***Second Lesson: She was wise in her assurance.*** Although she
   was surrounded by chaos, the wise woman untangled her reactions

Read

from her circumstances, and so her response was not chaotic. Instead, she focused on what was true — about herself, her city, and her attacker. Her assurance was grounded in truth rather than her circumstances.

+ If you were to stand in the reality of the circumstances that are battering the walls of your life right now, what *untruths* might they lead you to believe — about yourself, your situation, God?

+ Lysa talked about how we can trump feelings with truth: "Just because you *feel* incapable, offended, insecure doesn't mean you need to *be* incapable, offended, insecure." What truths might you use to trump the untruths you just identified? For example, Lysa's son Jackson chose to stand in the truth that the same God who had delivered him from an orphanage would still be there for him as he applied to college.

6. ***Third Lesson: She was wise in her advice.*** Even within a city recognized for its wisdom, the woman of Abel Beth Maakah had a sterling reputation for wisdom. People had watched her practicing wisdom in her everyday decisions. So when it mattered most — in this time of crisis — she didn't have to try to convince people her advice was wise. They trusted her.

+ Wisdom is like a muscle; if we want it to be strong in preparation for extraordinary circumstances, we have to give it regular workouts in ordinary circumstances. Overall, how would you describe your "wisdom workouts"? For example, what daily and routine settings give you the best opportunities to train your wisdom muscle?

❄ Because of what they witnessed in the wise woman's daily decisions, the people of Abel Beth Maakah came to trust her — and she saved their lives as a result. Whose trust would you most like to have when it comes to your ability to make wise decisions? Share the reasons for your response.

OPTIONAL DISCUSSION:
BECOMING A BEST YES GROUP (15 MINUTES)

If your group meets for two hours,
use this discussion as part of your meeting.

∾

Now that we're in the second session of our study, it's important to pray for each other through any challenges we may be facing. Spend a few moments discussing how you may be struggling in your approach, assurance, or advice. Feel free to share triumphs in those areas as well. Then pray for one another, noting any special requests.

INDIVIDUAL ACTIVITY:
What I Want to Remember (2 minutes)

Complete this activity on your own.

1. Briefly review the outline and any notes you took.
2. In the space below, write down the most significant thing you gained in this session—from the teaching, activities, or discussions.

What I want to remember from this session ...

CLOSING PRAYER

Close your time together with prayer. Ask God to lead you as you follow in the steps of the wise woman of Abel and practice wisdom this week in your approach, your assurance, and your advice.

GO DEEPER WITH *THE BEST YES*

For additional teaching and insights, read the following chapters in *The Best Yes* book if you haven't already done so:

4. Sometimes I Make It All So Complicated
5. God's Words, Ways, and Wonder
6. Chase Down That Decision

Wise Up

WEEK 2 READING WORKSHEET

If you're participating in the optional group challenge to read through the book of Proverbs, use this worksheet to help you keep track of your reading. If you'd like, use the space below to make notes and to reflect on what you read this week.

❑ Proverbs 8   ❑ Proverbs 11

❑ Proverbs 9   ❑ Proverbs 12

❑ Proverbs 10   ❑ Proverbs 13

What verses, words, or phrases stand out most to you? Why?

Knowledge

is wisdom that comes

from acquiring truth.

Insight

is wisdom that comes

from living out the truth we acquire.

Discernment

is wisdom that comes

from the Holy Spirit's reminders

of that knowledge and insight.

MINUTE
WISDOM

Session 2

Personal Study

WISDOM: AN EXPRESSION OF LOVE

> Discerning what is best is something we're capable of doing as we layer knowledge and depth of insight into our lives.
>
> *The Best Yes*, page 35

1. When you think of the characteristics of someone who consistently makes wise decisions, what words or phrases come to mind? Write down four to six. For example: *patience, intelligence, discernment,* etc.

   In the decisions and challenges you routinely face from day to day, which of these characteristics do you wish you had more of? How do you imagine your life and your decisions might be different if you could grow in this trait?

2. In his letter to the church at Philippi, the apostle Paul describes what he considers the foundational characteristic required for wisdom:

> And this is my prayer: that your love may abound more and more in knowledge and depth of insight, so that you may be able to discern what is best and may be pure and blameless for the day of Christ.
>
> (Philippians 1:9 – 10 NIV)

For Paul, the components of wisdom — knowledge, insight, and discernment — are first of all expressions of love.

How does thinking of wisdom primarily as an expression of love influence your perspective on what it means to be a wise person?

What connections, or disconnections, do you recognize between wisdom as an expression of love and the trait you identified in question 1?

> Is it loving to say no?
>   It feels more loving to say yes.
>
> *The Best Yes*, page 55

3. If we think of wisdom as an expression of love, that might lead us to conclude it is "wise" to say yes to every request. But Paul's famous love passage in 1 Corinthians 13 offers a caution:

> If I speak with human eloquence and angelic ecstasy but don't love, I'm nothing but the creaking of a rusty gate.
>
> If I speak God's Word with power, revealing all his mysteries and making everything plain as day, and if I have faith that says to a mountain, "Jump," and it jumps, but I don't love, I'm nothing.
>
> If I give everything I own to the poor and even go to the stake to be burned as a martyr, but I don't love, I've gotten nowhere. So, no matter what I say, what I believe, and what I do, I'm bankrupt without love.
>
> (1 Corinthians 13:1 – 3 MSG)

Paul describes some amazing expressions of faith, but he concludes that none of them count for anything if they're done without love. Without love, even saying yes to every request simply leaves us bankrupt. There's no wisdom in that.

Briefly recall a time recently when you said a yes that caused you to become worn out to a point where your attitude wasn't loving.

In what ways did your decision bankrupt you, leaving you feeling "less than" or diminished? For example: in your attitude, your relationships, your pace of life, etc.?

If you had that decision to make over again, what would be the most loving thing to do?

> The ways of God insist on an attitude of love. Therefore, my ways should reflect an attitude of love. Not a ragged, rushed, and rash attitude due to overactivity. Is it loving to say no? *Absolutely*, if doing so protects and preserves a loving attitude for the part of this assignment that is mine.
>
> *The Best Yes*, page 57

4. Having an attitude of love is not so much about always saying yes or even always saying no. It's about learning to say yes to those things that are truly meant to be our assignment — which requires saying no to those things that aren't. Then we can say yes not because we're guilted into saying yes. Or pressured into saying yes. Or saying yes by default because we couldn't figure out how to say no. Instead, we sense God's loving invitation to say yes.

Briefly recall a time recently when you said a loving yes — a yes to something, even a small something, you felt God was inviting you to. How did the experience of this yes differ from the yes you identified in question 3? What helped you to recognize it as your assignment?

What, if anything, did you have to say no to in order to say a loving yes to this invitation?

In what ways did your decision enrich you or those you served? How did it stretch you and help you to grow? For example: in your attitude, your relationships, your pace of life, etc.?

What loving yes do you sense God may be inviting you to consider in the week ahead?

5. Read Psalm 86:11 – 13, which describes the psalmist's desire to learn from God and to follow in God's ways. Use the psalm as a reference for writing your own prayer. Express to God your desire to learn from Him, and ask Him for the specific guidance you need. Praise and thank Him for His love, the foundation of all wisdom.

Session 2

Personal Study

CHASE DOWN THAT DECISION

The decisions we make today matter. Every decision points us in the direction we are about to travel. No decision is an isolated choice. It's a chain of events. So we've got to get good at chasing down our decisions. We need to look ahead to see where they will take us — and make sure that's really where we want to go. It's wisdom that comes straight from the book of Proverbs:

> A prudent person foresees danger and takes precautions. The simpleton goes blindly on and suffers the consequences.
>
> (Proverbs 22:3 NLT)

To get an idea of what it looks like to apply this principle even in the small decisions of everyday life, read the personal story Lysa shares in "Chasing Down Lattes." Use the story as a reference for the questions that follow.

CHASING DOWN LATTES

The other day, one of my friends asked me if I wanted to try her caramel-crunch-latte-love-something-fancy-with-whip-on-the-top. Yes, please. I would very much like to try that. But I

---

didn't. Why? Because I know myself very well. I won't crave something I never try. But if I try a sugary delish, I will crave said sugary delish. I will not just want a sip. I will want a whole one to myself. And then I will want a whole one to myself several times a week. So, let me chase down this decision.

I found out that drink has 560 calories. If I get in the habit of having three of those per week for the next year and change nothing about my current eating and exercising habits, I will take in an additional 87,360 calories. Thirty-five hundred calories equals one pound of fat. So, give or take how my body chemistry may process all this, according to math alone, I am set to gain about twenty-five pounds during this next year. When I chase down that decision, I refuse sips of drinks like these.

People laugh sometimes when I tell them this little process of mine and say, "Well you're just a disciplined person." Not really. Did you catch that part about how a sip for me would lead to enjoying this treat three times a week? I'm not really disciplined. I'm just determined — determined not to go places I don't want to go simply because I didn't take time to honestly evaluate. I've felt the heavy weight of regret and I don't want to return there.

I recognize some things happen to us that are beyond our control. But there's a whole lot that happens simply because we don't know how powerful it is to chase down a decision.

The Best Yes, pages 68, 70

In which of the following areas of life do you need to make a decision?

- ❑ *Physical*: food, exercise, rest, medical care, etc.
- ❑ *Financial*: earning, giving, saving, spending, debt, margin, etc.
- ❑ *Emotional*: contentment, healing, peace of mind, etc.

❑ *Spiritual*: putting God first, time alone with God, prayer, study, etc.
❑ *Relational*: spouse, kids, extended family, friends, colleagues, neighbors, etc.
❑ *Other*: _____

Circle one of the items you checked and use it as a focus for the remainder of this activity.

Using the prompts below, chase down your decision. Write your responses in the designated places on the diagram that follows.

+ **My decision.** Briefly identify a challenge or decision you face in the area of life you circled.

+ **Identify potential dangers.** One of the first things Lysa did with her latte decision was to consider the potential dangers — in this case, her self-defeating tendency to crave a sugary delish. What self-defeating tendencies or other potential dangers are you aware of in connection with the situation you identified?

+ **Face the facts.** Next, Lysa gathered some facts, specifically, the calorie count of the latte. What are the facts you know or could research about the situation you identified?

+ **Add it up.** Once Lysa had the facts, she chased down her decision by adding them up. Imagine making this same decision over and over. Adding up the cumulative impact of this decision will help you see its compounding effect.

+ **Take precautions.** After adding it up, the next step is to take precautions. For Lysa, that meant not taking a sip of her friend's latte. What precautions might you need to take to avoid negative consequences in your decision?

+ **Get perspective.** Now that you see where this decision will take you, ask yourself this question: "Is this where I really want to go?" If not, back up and change course by changing your decision.

When you are done working through your diagram, ask God for the additional guidance or strength you need in order to take the next step with your decision.

My Decision

Add It Up

Take Precautions

Session 2

Personal Study

TEN TIMES WISE

Briefly identify a situation for which you need wisdom to discern a Best Yes in the near future.

Read through the ten verses from Proverbs on the following page. Check the box next to any verse that might relate to your issue. Now consider how the verse or verses you checked might apply to your situation and write down any connections you recognize.

Make the verse or verses you checked the focus of your prayer. Ask God to help you apply this wisdom as you seek to make a Best Yes choice.

TEN PROVERBS

❑ Those who guard their lips preserve their lives, but those who speak rashly will come to ruin (Proverbs 13:3 NIV).

❑ He who walks with wise men will be wise. But the companion of fools will be destroyed (Proverbs 13:20 NKJV).

❑ Love prospers when a fault is forgiven, but dwelling on it separates close friends (Proverbs 17:9 NLT).

❑ He holds success in store for the upright, he is a shield to those whose walk is blameless (Proverbs 2:7 NIV).

❑ If you listen to constructive criticism, you will be at home among the wise (Proverbs 15:31 NLT).

❑ Whoever is patient has great understanding, but one who is quick-tempered displays folly (Proverbs 14:29 NIV).

❑ Wealth from get-rich-quick schemes quickly disappears; wealth from hard work grows over time (Proverbs 13:11 NLT).

❑ The one who hates good counsel will reap failure and ruin, but the one who reveres God's instruction will be rewarded (Proverbs 13:13 The Voice).

❑ Let love and faithfulness never leave you; bind them around your neck, write them on the tablet of your heart (Proverbs 3:3 NIV).

❑ A gentle answer turns away wrath, but a harsh word stirs up anger (Proverbs 15:1 NIV).

Practice Wisdom

Get all the advice and instruction you can,
so you will be wise the rest of your life.
Proverbs 19:20 NLT

Recommended reading prior to the meeting:
The Best Yes book, chapters 7 – 9

GROUP DISCUSSION:
Checking In (5 minutes)

If your group meets for two hours, allow 15 minutes
for this discussion.

A key part of getting to know God better is sharing your journey with others. Before watching the video, briefly check in with each other about your experiences since the last session. For example:

* What insights did you discover in the personal study, reading through Proverbs, or in the chapters you read from *The Best Yes* book?
* How did the last session impact your daily life or your relationship with God?
* What questions would you like to ask the other members of your group?

VIDEO:
Practice Wisdom (18 minutes)

Play the video segment for Session 3. As you watch, use the outline provided to follow along or to take additional notes on anything that stands out to you.

Notes

Everyday challenges make it so tough to live up to the kind of woman I want to be — the kind of woman God wants me to be.

According to 1 Kings 3:12, Solomon had great wisdom. Yet he also had 700 wives and 300 concubines and eventually worshiped false gods.

Wisdom must be practiced; it is a process of acquisition and application.

We acquire wisdom by going where wisdom gathers and not where it scatters.

Ashley is an athlete. She has to show up to practice. She has to acquire the wisdom of her sport and then apply it as she shows up to practice every day.

Ashley made it, and we can make it too. We can go where wisdom gathers.

"He who guards his lips guards his life, but he who speaks rashly will come to ruin" (Proverbs 13:3 NIV 1984).

If we want to know God's direction, we have to listen to His instruction.

Key verse: Psalm 90:12

> "Teach us to number our days, that we may gain a heart of wisdom" (NIV).
> "So teach us to number our days, that we may apply our hearts unto wisdom" (KJV).
> "So teach us to number our days, that we may present to You a heart of wisdom" (NASB).

Teach us to number our days. Make our days count. Make our decisions count so we will have a heart of wisdom that we have practiced over and over. Then when it matters most, we too can get above the obstacles that come our way.

"Set your hearts on things above, where Christ is, seated at the right hand of God. Set your minds on things above, not on earthly things" (Colossians 3:1 – 2 NIV).

We have to:

- Count our days.
- Listen to the voice of wisdom.
- Gather the tools of our practice.
- Set our heart and mind on things above. Say, "I am a wise woman. Therefore, it is possible for me to acquire wisdom that lifts me above this obstacle and apply wisdom as I set my heart and my mind on things above."

In our pursuit of acquiring wisdom, there will be highs and lows, but most importantly, we just need to show up daily for practice.

This Week: Acquire and apply wisdom to a decision in which you have some fear about moving forward. It might be a complex decision or one that requires courage in order to say a Best Yes. Make this an opportunity to "show up to practice" and stretch your wisdom muscles.[*]

My Thoughts:

---

[*]   See the Session 3 personal study for additional guidance with this assignment.

GROUP DISCUSSION:
Video Debrief (5 minutes)

> If your group meets for two hours, allow 10 minutes
> for this discussion.

1. What part of the teaching had the most impact on you?

Practice, Practice, Practice (15 minutes)

> If your group meets for two hours, allow 30 minutes
> for this discussion.

2. Lysa told a story about how her daughter Ashley was determined to become a pole-vaulter and kept showing up for hours and hours of practice even when she didn't seem to be making progress.

    * When you were growing up, what did you devote hours and hours of practice to? For example: building your skills in a childhood game, learning to drive, playing a sport, learning an instrument, etc.

    ✦ Author Malcolm Gladwell writes, "Practice isn't the thing you do once you're good. It's the thing you do that makes you good."[1] When you were just beginning and weren't yet very skilled, what motivated you to keep at it? What kept you from quitting?

3. It's tempting to think that wisdom might be one of those things that comes more naturally to some people than others, but learning wisdom is a lot like learning other skills — the only way to get better is to practice. In the 1990s, a Florida State University psychologist named Anders Ericsson published research demonstrating how expert performers such as musicians and athletes acquired their superior abilities. What he discovered was that natural talent wasn't the determining factor. Instead, superior performance came from what he called "deliberate practice."

> You don't get benefits from mechanical repetition, but by adjusting your execution over and over to get closer to your goal. You have to tweak the system by pushing, allowing for more errors at first as you increase your limits.... The more time expert performers are able to invest in deliberate practice with full concentration, the further developed and refined their performance.[2]

    ✦ When it comes to learning and practicing wisdom, how do you feel about the idea of pushing yourself and allowing for more errors at first?

    ✦ If deliberate practice requires full concentration, what do you think it might mean to devote full concentration to learning

---

1 Malcolm Gladwell, *Outliers: The Story of Success* (New York: Little Brown and Company, 2008), 42.
2 Quoted in Daniel Goleman, *Focus: The Hidden Driver of Excellence* (New York: HarperCollins, 2013), 163, 165.

wisdom? (As a reference, consider any connections you might make to how you have experienced full concentration in learning any other new skill.)

* One additional characteristic Ericsson identified was that expert performers come to love practice and actually seek it out. Overall, how would you describe your "love level" when it comes to practicing wisdom? For example, do you tend to associate the need for wisdom primarily with solving problems and seek it out only when you have to? Or are you more likely to seek out opportunities to practice wisdom and to enjoy the process of learning? Share the reasons for your response.

Acquire and Apply (15 minutes)

If your group meets for two hours, allow 30 minutes for this discussion.

4. When Ashley was learning to pole vault, she listened to the voice of her coach and made constant adjustments in order to get closer to her goal. In his research, this process is what psychologist Anders Ericsson described as a feedback loop. Thousands of years ago, the writer of Proverbs said it this way:

> Get all the advice and instruction you can, so you will be wise the rest of your life.

> (Proverbs 19:20 NLT)

> Listen to the words of the wise; apply your heart to
> my instruction.
>   (Proverbs 22:17 NIV)

✦ If you could have a wisdom coach, someone with an expert eye who could help you make constant adjustments to get closer to your wisdom goals, how would you want that person to help you? On what practices or skills would you most like to have that person's advice and instruction?

✦ How do you respond to the idea of seeking out "all the advice and instruction you can"? For example, does it feel burdensome—like one more thing you don't have the time, energy, or desire to do? Or does it feel life-giving, like something you would look forward to and enjoy? Share the reasons for your response.

✦ Briefly recall an experience in which someone coached you or gave you guidance that helped you to make a better decision. How specifically did this person's feedback help you? What adjustments did you make that strengthened your wisdom muscle or improved your decision making?

5. If Ashley had only listened to her coach and applied his instructions on competition days, she would never have developed her skills enough to advance. It was her faithfulness on all the in-between

days — the practice days — that enabled her to improve her skills. The same principle is true for us. If we want God's direction for our decisions, we must be willing to follow his instructions not just in the extraordinary situations but also in all the in-between ones.

On the video, Lysa shared a story about one of those in-between moments for her. Someone had hurt her feelings, and her natural inclination was to respond with a comeback. Instead, she applied the wisdom of God's instruction to guard her lips (Proverbs 13:3), and God's direction enabled her to change her response.

* How would you describe the kind of decisions you routinely struggle with in your in-between moments? For example, is it a challenge to make wise decisions about using words, like the decision Lysa described? Or is your challenge more likely to be about scheduling decisions? Relational decisions? Strategic decisions about personal or work issues?

* In Lysa's situation, her natural inclination was a quick comeback. What's your natural inclination in the kinds of situations you just described?

* Overall, would you say your challenge tends to be more about a lack of direction (not having the wisdom you need), or about a lack of follow-through (not applying the wisdom you have)? Share the reasons for your response.

✦ Knowing that you will likely face another in-between moment soon, what do you feel you need most from God in order to follow His instructions and practice wisdom?

**OPTIONAL DISCUSSION:
BECOMING A BEST YES GROUP (15 MINUTES)**

If your group meets for two hours, use this discussion as part of your meeting.

𝓎

Briefly reflect on what you've learned and experienced together in this study so far.

- How has learning more about wisdom and making Best Yes decisions influenced you or changed your decision making?

- Since the first session, what shifts have you noticed in yourself in terms of how you relate to the group? For example: do you feel more or less guarded, understood, challenged, encouraged, connected, etc.?

- Based on the prayer requests from last session, share any updates or answered prayer within the group.

INDIVIDUAL ACTIVITY:
What I Want to Remember (2 minutes)

Complete this activity on your own.

1. Briefly review the outline and any notes you took.
2. In the space below, write down the most significant thing you gained in this session — from the teaching, activities, or discussions.

What I want to remember from this session ...

CLOSING PRAYER

Close your time together with prayer. Ask God to help you listen to His voice — the voice of wisdom — and give you a heart that is eager to practice wisdom in the decisions and challenges you face this week.

GO DEEPER WITH *THE BEST YES*

For additional teaching and insights, read the following chapters in *The Best Yes* book if you haven't already done so:

7. Analysis Paralysis
8. Consider the Trade
9. Show Up to Practice

Wise Up

WEEK 3 READING WORKSHEET

If you're participating in the optional group challenge to read through the book of Proverbs, use this worksheet to help you keep track of your reading. If you'd like, use the space below to make notes and to reflect on what you read this week.

❑ Proverbs 14   ❑ Proverbs 17
❑ Proverbs 15   ❑ Proverbs 18
❑ Proverbs 16   ❑ Proverbs 19

What verses, words, or phrases stand out most to you? Why?

That daily stuff—those responsibilities that seem more like distractions—those things we want to rush and just get through to get on with the better and bigger assignments of life—those things that are unnoticed places of service? They are the very experiences from which we unlock the riches of wisdom. We've got to practice wisdom in the everyday places of our lives.

Session 3

Personal Study

DECISIONS, DECISIONS

> Maybe you have been there. A decision needs to be made. You ponder and pray. You research and get other people's opinions. You analyze the hows and what-ifs. You desperately want to know which is the one right decision to make. The perfect move. The will of God. And suddenly you find yourself hanging … paralyzed from moving forward.
>
> *The Best Yes*, pages 77–78

1. When you have to make a decision for which it seems there is no clear answer, what fears are most likely to keep you from moving forward?

   ❏ The unknown
   ❏ Failure
   ❏ Getting hurt
   ❏ Stepping out of God's will
   ❏ What others may think
   ❏ Experiencing a loss I can't overcome

   ❏ Rejection
   ❏ Disappointing someone
   ❏ Missing out on something better
   ❏ Making the wrong decision
   ❏ Being misunderstood
   ❏ Other: _____

How would you describe the *background* for the fears you checked? In other words, what previous experiences in similar circumstances contribute to your fears?

Now look ahead and consider the *foreground* for your fears. When you think about following through on a decision, what do you see on the horizon? For example: *I feel like I'll set off a chain of events that will leave me in a bad place and without options. If I miss God's will, I'll never get back to the place I could and should have been. I will have to deal with the fallout of disappointing people, which will make my life hard.*

Briefly identify a current situation in which you have some fear about moving ahead with a decision. (If you can't identify a current situation, think back to a previous situation in which fear made it difficult for you to move ahead.) Use this situation as your focus for the remaining questions.

I do think we should fear stepping out of God's will. But if you desire to please God with the decision you make and afterward it proves to be a mistake, it's an error not an end.

The Best Yes, page 79

2. An *error* is an unintentional mistake; an *end* is a termination. When considering the potential outcome of a difficult decision, it's important to distinguish the errors from the ends in our thinking.

Use the prompts below and on the next page to identify one or two ends you might be thinking of in your situation, and then transition them into errors instead. An example has been provided.

Example

My fear: Stepping out of God's will

*Thinking of a potential mistake as an **end** means:* If I step out of God's will, I will never recover from the consequences or experience God's best for me.

*Thinking of a potential mistake as an **error** means:* If I step out of God's will, I may experience consequences but I can learn from my mistake (which is wisdom!) and trust that God will redeem it.

෴

My fear:

*Thinking of a potential mistake as an **end** means:*

*Thinking of a potential mistake as an **error** means:*

My fear:

*Thinking of a potential mistake as an **end** means:*

*Thinking of a potential mistake as an **error** means:*

If I'm trusting myself, I will stare at all the possible ways I could fail. If I'm trusting God, I will stare at all the possible ways He'll use this whether I fail or succeed.

When I stare at failure, I'll fear it. I'll convince myself it's the worst thing that could happen. And I'll stay stuck. But when I stare at all the possible ways God can use this whether I succeed or fail, I'll face my decision. I'll convince myself that it's better to step out and find out than stay stuck.

The Best Yes, page 83

3. In order to practice wisdom in Best Yes decisions, we have to set our sights on growing our faith, not fearing our failures or the errors we could make. We do this when we apply *thought* and *prayer* to our decisions and then *trust* God with the outcome.

    Use the following continuums to get a snapshot of how you're doing in growing your faith with the situation you identified in question 1. Place an X on each of the continuums below to indicate your response.

Thought

I have given little or no
thought to this decision

I have given a great deal
of thought to this decision.

Prayer

I have devoted little or
no prayer to this decision.

I have devoted a great
deal of prayer to this decision.

Trust

I have not entrusted
the outcome of this
decision — whatever
it is — to God.

I have fully entrusted the
outcome of this decision —
whatever it is — to God.

Circle the word above the continuum on which you placed the X farthest to the left. What makes this aspect of faith and decision making harder for you right now?

Entrusting the outcome of a decision to God means "we accept that we do not have in ourselves—in our own 'heart, soul, mind, and strength'—the wherewithal to make *this* come out right, whatever 'this' is."[3] Therefore, we trust that whatever the outcome is, God will use it for our good and His glory (Romans 8:28).

What is it you are trying hardest to make "come out right" in your decision?

What are some of the ways God might use the outcome of your decision, whether or not it comes out the way you hope it will?

4. Here is a great truth from Scripture to help us entrust ourselves to God while practicing wisdom and moving ahead with hard decisions:

> Trust in the LORD with all your heart; do not depend on your own understanding. Seek his will in all you do, and he will show you which path to take.
> (Proverbs 3:5–6 NLT)

For a fresh perspective on this familiar passage, read it again from *The Message*:

> Trust GOD from the bottom of your heart; don't try to figure out everything on your own. Listen for GOD's voice in everything you do, everywhere you go; he's the one who will keep you on track.
> (Proverbs 3:5–6 MSG)

---

3 Dallas Willard, *Renovation of the Heart: Putting on the Character of Christ* (Colorado Springs: NavPress, 2002), 209.

These verses make it clear that the opposite of trusting God is depending on our own understanding — trying to figure out everything on our own.

What small steps of faith might you take in each of the following ways to help you focus on growing your faith rather than fearing failure in your decision?

I can trust in the Lord with all of my heart by . . .

I can avoid trying to figure out everything on my own by . . .

I can seek God's will and listen to His voice in all I do by . . .

5. Read Psalm 62:5 – 8, in which David encourages his soul to rest in God. Use the psalm as a reference for writing a message of hope and encouragement to your own soul. Then turn your attention to God in prayer. Ask for His help in any places where you feel stuck and unable to move forward. Entrust yourself and the outcome of your decisions to Him. Thank Him for being a mighty rock you can depend on at all times.

Session 3

Personal Study

CONSIDER THE TRADE, MAKE THE RELEASE

Virtually every decision we make requires some kind of trade-off—in order to say yes to one thing, we have to say no to another. But sometimes it's a struggle to make the release and let go, even in the routine, everyday decisions. See if you relate to any of these examples:

- *I stay up late (watching television, surfing the Internet, scrolling through social media, etc.) even though I know I need more sleep. I refuse to release whatever I'm doing in order to get the rest I need. The next day I am tired, grumpy, and short-tempered.*

- *I put off making decisions I know I need to make. It might be cleaning out my closet, saying no to an invitation, or committing to budget changes in order to pay down debt. I delay, delay, delay so I don't have to release whatever making the decision might cost me. In the meantime, I live with the stress of not making the decision—a messy closet, guilt for avoiding the person who extended the invitation, the weight of mounting debt.*

- *I want to be healthier—yet sugar is my downfall. I know I need to give it up, at least for a season, but I refuse to release it. I justify a small Frappuccino one day, a few cookies the next, a piece of cake at the office party the day after that, and on it goes. Then I live with the regret, guilt, and disappointment of not feeling good about myself and failing to reach my goals.*

Use the chart below to briefly reflect on two or three releases you're finding it difficult to make right now, and how they might be robbing you of peace. (An example has been provided.)

What I Refuse to Release	How It Robs Me of Peace
I stay up late, and refuse to release watching just one more show on Hulu or Netflix.	*The next day I am tired, grumpy, and short-tempered, which often leads to unnecessary problems with family or coworkers. It also makes it hard to concentrate and do my best work.*

We aren't in the habit of release. Why? Because of the fear of missing out on some things. But in the process we miss out on the best things. If we want to grow in wisdom and establish a pattern of discerning Best Yes answers, we must consider the trade and make the release.

There are plenty of cautionary examples in Scripture that show how refusing to release gets people into trouble.

- *Eve.* By refusing to release her desire for the forbidden fruit, Eve missed out on the best things in paradise (Genesis 3).
- *Esau.* When he refused to release his immediate demand for some stew, Esau missed out on inheriting his birthright (Genesis 25:29 – 34).
- *Moses.* By refusing to release his fear that just speaking to the rock as God commanded would actually bring forth water, Moses struck the rock instead and missed out on entering the Promised Land (Numbers 20:1 – 12).
- *David.* When he refused to release his inappropriate desire for Bathsheba, David set off a chain of sinful events, including adultery and murder. As a result, he suffered the tragic loss of a child (2 Samuel 11:2 – 27, 12:14).

Choose one of the biblical examples and read the corresponding Scriptures. What connections might you make between the biblical character's story and the release challenges you identified on the chart? For example, how do you relate to that person's refusal to release?

If you were able to consider the trade and make the release, what are some of the "best things" you hope you might experience?

Read Proverbs 4:25 – 27, which encourages God's people to keep their eyes focused on what lies ahead — the best things. This is wisdom. Talk to God about the releases you're struggling to make, and ask Him to help you be steadfast in pursuing the best things your heart truly desires.

Session 3

Personal Study

TEN TIMES WISE

Briefly identify a situation for which you need wisdom to discern a Best Yes in the near future.

Read through the ten verses from Proverbs on the following page. Check the box next to any verse that might relate to your issue. Now consider how the verse or verses you checked might apply to your situation and write down any connections you recognize.

Make the verse or verses you checked the focus of your prayer. Ask God to help you apply this wisdom as you seek to make a Best Yes choice.

TEN PROVERBS

❑ The wise are cautious and avoid danger; fools plunge ahead with reckless confidence (Proverbs 14:16 NLT).

❑ Give careful thought to the paths for your feet and be steadfast in all your ways. Do not turn to the right or the left; keep your foot from evil (Proverbs 4:26 – 27 NIV).

❑ Plans fail for lack of counsel, but with many advisers they succeed (Proverbs 15:22 NIV).

❑ Pride goes before destruction, and a haughty spirit before a fall (Proverbs 16:18 NKJV).

❑ A troublemaker plants seeds of strife; gossip separates the best of friends (Proverbs 16:28 NLT).

❑ Starting a quarrel is like breaching a dam; so drop the matter before a dispute breaks out (Proverbs 17:14 NIV).

❑ Whoever heeds discipline shows the way to life, but whoever ignores correction leads others astray (Proverbs 10:17 NIV).

❑ Fools have no desire to learn; they would much rather give their own opinion (Proverbs 18:2 CEV).

❑ Slack habits and sloppy work are as bad as vandalism (Proverbs 18:9 MSG).

❑ The wise store up knowledge, but the mouth of a fool invites ruin (Proverbs 10:14 NIV).

Predetermine Your Best Yes

Let's go at once to take the land …
We can certainly conquer it!
Numbers 13:30 NLT

Recommended reading prior to the meeting:
The Best Yes book, chapters 10 – 12

GROUP DISCUSSION:
Checking In (5 minutes)

If your group meets for two hours, allow 15 minutes
for this discussion.

A key part of getting to know God better is sharing your journey with others. Before watching the video, briefly check in with each other about your experiences since the last session. For example:

+ What insights did you discover in the personal study, reading through Proverbs, or in the chapters you read from *The Best Yes* book?
+ How did the last session impact your daily life or your relationship with God?
+ What questions would you like to ask the other members of your group?

VIDEO:
Predetermine Your Best Yes (12 minutes)

Play the video segment for Session 4. As you watch, use the outline provided to follow along or to take additional notes on anything that stands out to you.

Notes

The good thing about a cliff is that you know where the edge is.

We live in this place of an overwhelming schedule and an underwhelmed soul because we're constantly dancing on the edge of the cliff.

The story of Joshua and Caleb helps us understand what it means to predetermine our Best Yes life.

> Moses sent twelve spies into the Promised Land to scout out what the land was like. Joshua and Caleb were among them.
>
> Ten spies came back and reported that there were giants and walls and armies.
>
> Joshua and Caleb had a different perspective: "Let's go at once to take the land. … We can certainly conquer it!" (Numbers 13:30 NLT).
>
> The people refused, and so they wandered in the desert for the next forty years.
>
> Forty years later, Caleb said, "I was forty years old when Moses, the servant of the LORD sent me … to explore the land. And I brought him back a report according to my convictions, but my brothers who went up with me made the hearts of the people melt with fear. I, however, followed the LORD my God wholeheartedly (Joshua 14:7 – 8 NIV 1984).
>
> Caleb's conviction was a fixed or firm belief.
>
> Caleb predetermined that God would help him conquer the land. Conquering the land was his Best Yes. He said yes to his convictions, which meant he had to say no to the popular opinion that the land was impossible to conquer.

If we predetermine that we are going to say yes to our Promised Land — our Best Yes life — we are going to have to say no to some people and opportunities. We have to say no to those things that don't fit the season we are in or the convictions of our heart.

One of my Best Yes decisions was to predetermine that Monday nights would be kept very special.

There are two different kinds of no — the small no and the big no. A small no is one I can quickly give when a competing request is made.

The White Cliffs of Dover are made of chalk and flint.

- ⚜ A small no is like writing in chalk; it doesn't leave a long-lasting impression.
- ⚜ When flint is struck, it can start a fire. Letting a decision slip away from you until it becomes a big no can cause so much more damage than a small no.

As you arrange your mind, your heart, and your schedule to accommodate your predetermined Best Yes, you'll experience the satisfaction of enjoying the view instead of fearing the edge.

This Week: Assignment 1: Predetermine your Best Yes activity and set your schedule accordingly. Quickly and kindly turn down anything that could send you over the edge. Assignment 2: Exercise the power of the small no.[*]

My Thoughts:

---

[*] See the Session 4 personal study for additional guidance in completing these assignments.

GROUP DISCUSSION:
Video Debrief (5 minutes)

If your group meets for two hours, allow 10 minutes
for this discussion.

1. What part of the teaching had the most impact on you?

Life on the Edge (13 minutes)

If your group meets for two hours, allow 26 minutes
for this discussion.

2. Too often, we live with an overwhelmed schedule and an underwhelmed soul because we're constantly dancing on the edge of the cliff. How would you describe the pace of your life right now? Mark an X or draw a stick figure on the cliff image below to indicate your response.

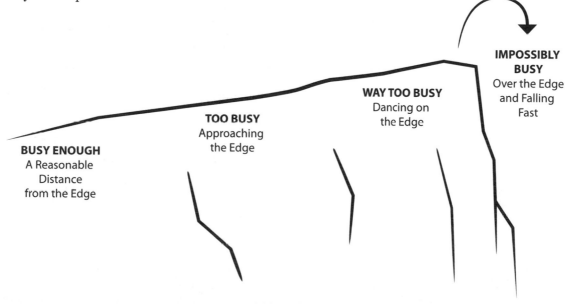

BUSY ENOUGH
A Reasonable
Distance
from the Edge

TOO BUSY
Approaching
the Edge

WAY TOO BUSY
Dancing on
the Edge

IMPOSSIBLY
BUSY
Over the Edge
and Falling
Fast

⚜ Where did you place yourself on the cliff? Briefly share your response with the group.

⚜ Lysa described how there is actually a blessing in a cliff because you know where your edge is and when you are about to go too far. How would you describe your edge? How do you know when you are getting too close to it?

3. Various cultures and communities have differing views on busyness. For example, some attach a high value to it and occasionally take it to extremes; others try to avoid it and place a higher value on balance or rest.

⚜ Overall, how would you describe the way your culture views busyness?

⚜ Within your community, would you say that the busier someone is, the more likely it is that they will be admired and considered important? Or is busyness more likely to cause a person to lose admiration and importance? Share any examples you can think of to illustrate your response.

❖ In what ways might you have to say no to the prevailing views of your culture or community in order to say yes to a sustainable pace of life?

Heart Convictions (23 minutes)

> If your group meets for two hours, allow 45 minutes for this discussion.

4. In the biblical story Lysa shared, Caleb had to say no to the prevailing views of his community in order to say yes to his convictions:

> I was forty years old when Moses, the servant of the Lord sent me ... to explore the land. And I brought him back a report according to my convictions, but my fellow Israelites who went up with me made the hearts of the people melt in fear. I, however, followed the Lord my God wholeheartedly.
> (Joshua 14:7 – 8)

Caleb's statement gives us a picture of two hearts: his own, and that of the people. When Caleb describes his "convictions," he uses the Hebrew word *lēbāb* (lay-bawb´), which means heart — he gave his report "according to my [heart]."[4] The word "wholeheartedly" in Hebrew means to be complete or full.[5] The picture we have of Caleb's heart is that it was undivided and filled with faith. Caleb's conviction made him certain of God's instructions to take the land.

In contrast, the people lost their conviction. Their hearts were both divided and disbelieving, melted by fear. The Hebrew word for "melted" means to be liquefied or drenched to the point of dissolving.[6] It's quite a contrast! One heart follows fear and dissolves; the other follows God and is filled with courage.

---

4 Alex Luc, "*lēbāb*," *Dictionary of Old Testament Theology and Exegesis*, vol. 2, Willem A. VanGemeren, gen. ed. (Grand Rapids: Zondervan, 1997), 749.

5 Miles V. Van Pelt and Walter C. Kaiser, Jr., "*ml´*," *Dictionary of Old Testament Theology and Exegesis*, vol. 2, Willem A. VanGemeren, gen. ed. (Grand Rapids: Zondervan, 1997), 939.

6 Robin Wakely, "*msh*," *Dictionary of Old Testament Theology and Exegesis*, vol. 2, Willem A. VanGemeren, gen. ed. (Grand Rapids: Zondervan, 1997), 997.

- Lysa used Caleb as an example of what it means to predetermine a Best Yes — to act on the convictions of God's instructions. How strong are the convictions of your heart right now when it comes to your pace of life and the way you make decisions about your time? For example, do you feel you can confidently say no when you need to, or do you struggle to do so?

- In the face of their challenges — giants, walls, and armies — the Israelites almost literally lost heart. Their convictions about God's instructions melted. When you think about the challenges you could face in predetermining a Best Yes, what might weaken your convictions or cause you to lose heart?

- If Caleb had been a yes man, going along with the crowd, he would never have entered the Promised Land. It was his whole-hearted conviction that God could be trusted that gave him courage to make a Best Yes decision instead. What do the fears you identified above reveal about what you most need from God in order to be courageous with this part of your life?

5. When Lysa wanted her home to be a place where her family could connect and others could receive love and nourishment, she had a choice: she could try each week to somehow find whatever time might be available in her busy schedule, or she could *predetermine* the time and protect it.

+ Are there choices you've already made to predetermine something on your schedule? If so, what enables you to protect that time? If not, what makes this kind of choice challenging for you right now?

+ Lysa's predetermined choice came from her desire for a welcoming home. What desires come to mind when you think of the things you want but can't seem to find time for?

+ Underwhelming her schedule on Monday nights enabled Lysa to overwhelm her soul by connecting with people she cared about. If you were able to predetermine time for one of the desires you identified, how do you hope it might feed your soul or enrich your life?

6. There are two different kinds of no — the small no and the big no. A small no is one we can give quickly. The big no is what happens when we put off saying the small no to the point that it becomes harder to give, is more painful than if it had been given earlier, or is now nearly impossible to give.

    + Sometimes we delay saying a small no even when we know it's the best response. What thoughts tend to go through your head when you choose to delay saying a small no? For example: *If I put it off, maybe this request will somehow go away so I won't have to deal with it.*

✦ How does switching things around and putting yourself in the shoes of the person making the request influence your perspective on the small no?

✦ If someone needed to say no to you, how might he or she do it in a respectful and loving way?

**OPTIONAL DISCUSSION:
BECOMING A BEST YES GROUP (10 MINUTES)**

If your group meets for two hours, use this discussion
as part of your meeting.

↬

- For what specific aspect of courage do you need your group to pray on your behalf?

    ❑ Courage to say a small no
    ❑ Courage to be more countercultural with busyness
    ❑ Courage in the face of a personal giant

- Write each person's name and contact information on a note card. Choose prayer partners for the week and use these cards to keep in touch throughout the week. Be sure to check in with your prayer partner with an encouraging call, text, or email.

INDIVIDUAL ACTIVITY:
What I Want to Remember (2 minutes)

Complete this activity on your own.

1. Briefly review the outline and any notes you took.
2. In the space below, write down the most significant thing you gained in this session — from the teaching, activities, or discussions.

What I want to remember from this session . . .

CLOSING PRAYER

Close your time together with prayer. Ask God to give you wisdom as you seek to predetermine a Best Yes this week.

GO DEEPER WITH *THE BEST YES*

For additional teaching and insights, read the following chapters in *The Best Yes* book if you haven't already done so:

10. Managing Demands Means Understanding Expectations
11. The Power of the Small No
12. The Awkward Disappointment of Saying No

Wise Up

WEEK 4 READING WORKSHEET

If you're participating in the optional group challenge to read through the book of Proverbs, use this worksheet to help you keep track of your reading. If you'd like, use the space below to make notes and to reflect on what you read this week.

❑ Proverbs 20   ❑ Proverbs 23
❑ Proverbs 21   ❑ Proverbs 24
❑ Proverbs 22   ❑ Proverbs 25

What verses, words, or phrases stand out most to you? Why?

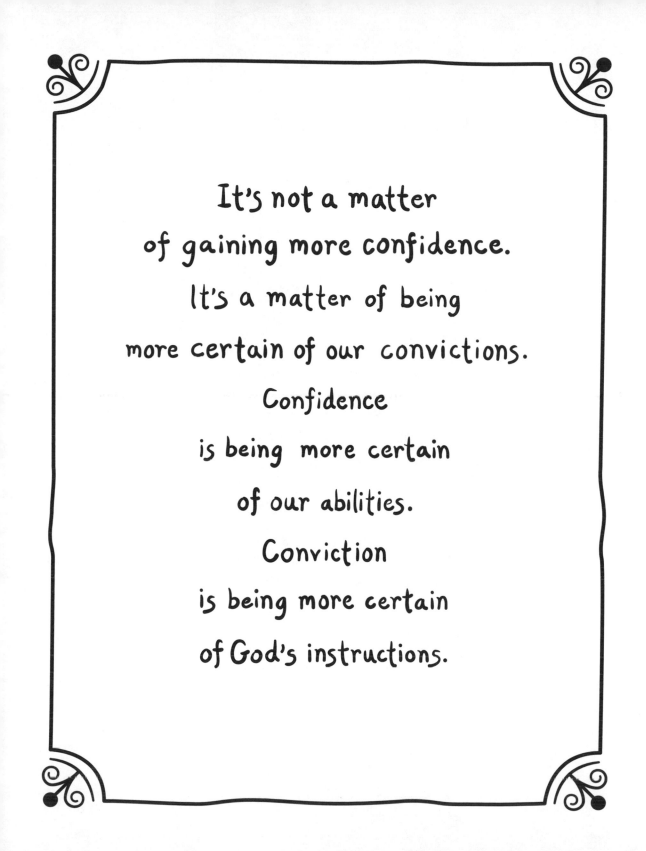

It's not a matter
of gaining more confidence.
It's a matter of being
more certain of our convictions.
Confidence
is being more certain
of our abilities.
Conviction
is being more certain
of God's instructions.

Session 4

Personal Study

THE ART OF SAYING NO

> A small no pushes through the resistance of awkwardness and disappointment because it's better to nip something early on. Early on, expectations and disappointments can be managed better with a small no. But the more we let things develop and progress, the harder the no becomes.
>
> *The Best Yes*, pages 126–127

1. What small no answers do you need to exercise in your life right now? Using the following chart, briefly identify two or three. Areas of life to consider might include invitations or requests from friends and family, people at church, neighbors, school teachers, colleagues, etc.

   For each no you identify, write down one or two ways it might get harder the longer you wait.

A Small No I Need to Say	How This No Might Get Harder the Longer I Wait

I've learned the best "no" answers are graciously honest.

The Best Yes, page 133

2. Even if you feel a little awkward about disappointing someone, you can still say a simple and graciously honest no. Here are a few examples:

   ✢ *While my heart wants to say yes, the reality of my time makes this a no.*
   ✢ *I'm sorry, but I'm not able to give this the attention it deserves.*
   ✢ *I would love to, but my previous commitments with _____ make this one of those seasons when I must decline lovely invitations. But thank you for thinking of me.*
   ✢ *It's difficult for me to say no, but I need to pass this time.*
   ✢ *Even though I would love to, this isn't something I have capacity for right now.*

Another option is to make a counter offer that *does* work for you: *I can't do* _____ *but I can do* _____. For example:

I'm not able to come on Mondays, but I would love to help you out. In order to keep better balance in my life, I've started scheduling Fridays as my service opportunity days. Let me know what part of your request can be done on a Friday and I'll be happy to help.

For each no you identified in question 1, choose one of the example statements and adapt it to your situation. As you write out your responses, resist any temptation to overexplain or to sugarcoat the truth. Follow the Lord's guidance in keeping it simple and honest:

> "Just say 'yes' and 'no.' When you manipulate words to get your own way, you do wrong."
> (Matthew 5:37 MSG)

Every yes answer comes with a list of expectations. If I don't know what those expectations are, I can't possibly meet them. So, it's crucial to identify the expectations before giving a yes answer.... I make a plan for what's realistic so I don't overextend myself.

The Best Yes, pages 116–117

3. Sometimes deciding whether or not to say no is fairly straightforward. But there are other times when it's much more challenging—especially when a great opportunity comes our way. Consider the story Lysa shares about how her friend Genia faced this kind of decision in "Evaluate the Opportunity."

EVALUATE THE OPPORTUNITY

My friend Genia has been an avid exercise girl her whole life. She's one of these people who absolutely gets excited about working out. I don't understand this. I work out to keep myself sane and try to manage my weight. I like the benefits, but I can't say I always like exercising.

Genia loves it. And she loves her local YMCA where she takes classes and spends hours sweating. For years, as she walked into her YMCA, she admired the pictures of the board members who run the business side of this gym. And she secretly hoped that one day they would ask her to be a board member.

Last week, she got the invite she's dreamed of for a long time. They asked her to consider being a board member. She was thrilled as she read the e-mail. Her heart pumped fast as a huge smile spread across her face.

Her first inclination was to shoot back a quick e-mail saying, "Yes, I'm incredibly honored you would ask me!" But she waited so she could take time to assess whether this exciting opportunity was a Best Yes for her in this season of her life.

Part of this assessment was carefully reading the attachment with all the expectations of a board member and the dates for the next two years' worth of meetings she'd be committing to attend.

(cont.)

As she placed that e-mail next to her calendar, her smile dimmed. God kept whispering other things to her heart in that quiet time of consideration. "Give the best of who you are to what you're already committed to."

For a couple of days, Genia kept thinking about what she felt the Lord was telling her about giving the best of herself to her prior commitments. She kept looking at all the dates and all the expectations. And here's where she landed:

The expected meetings didn't match the amount of time she had to give. They would quickly have become an unrealistic expectation for her, and the thrill of being asked would quickly wear into a dread of disappointment. Her limited ability to serve would become a disappointment to herself, to them, and to the other commitments to which she already promised her time.

So, she graciously declined this opportunity.

As we processed this situation a few days later, she was so thankful she'd clearly understood the expectations beforehand. Indeed, evaluation saved her a lot of frustration.

The Best Yes, pages 122–123

Pick an opportunity decision you are in the midst of making right now and briefly describe it below.

Use the following questions to help you assess whether or not the expectations you'd be agreeing to with this yes are really realistic.

* It may feel thrilling to say yes to this now, but how will this yes feel two weeks, two months, and six months from now?

* Do any of the expectations attached to this yes feel forced or frantic?

* Could any part of this yes be tied to people pleasing and allowing that desire to skew your judgment of what's realistic and unrealistic?

* Which wise (older, grounded in God's Word, more experienced, and more mature) people in your life think this is a good idea?

* Are there any facts you might try to avoid or hide when discussing this opportunity with your wise advisers? If so, list them below.

> Unrealistic expectations become unmet expectations. And unmet expectations are like kindling wood — it only takes but a spark of frustration to set them ablaze and burn those involved.... If there is a lingering list of unrealistic expectations, they must be discussed and negotiated through until they either become realistic or get dropped from the opportunity at hand.
>
> *The Best Yes*, pages 120–121

4. When making a decision about an opportunity, we have to consider it from all angles. Identifying potential unrealistic expectations helps you to know what to discuss before saying yes — before there is a gap between what you can deliver and the expectations of others. Use the questions on the following chart to consider your opportunity from five angles — time, ability, money, passion, and season.

Questions to Consider	My Responses
My time: Is the schedule or time commitment required in line with the time I have to invest?	
My ability: Do I have the necessary skills and abilities to carry out the functions of this opportunity?	
My money: Can I afford the financial responsibilities that come along with this opportunity? Or, is the potential income generated from this opportunity worth the time I must invest?	
My passion: Do the responsibilities of this opportunity evoke a sense of fulfillment and eager expectation or a sense of dread and avoidance?	
My season: Is the timing right? Is there something that must take a higher priority during this season of my life?	

Based on your chart and your responses to question 3, what are your observations about this opportunity? Overall, would you say it is realistic or unrealistic?

Read Psalm 119:29 – 32, in which the psalmist asks God to, "Keep me from lying to myself" (NLT) and affirms his determination to be faithful. Use the psalm as a reference for writing your own prayer. Acknowledge any concerns you have about the no answers you need to give. Ask God to broaden your understanding of the situations you face and to give you courage to say no simply, graciously, and honestly.

Session 4

Personal Study

PREDETERMINE YOUR BEST YES

If you want to say yes to your Best Yes life, you'll need to say no to some things that don't fit the season you are in or don't fit the convictions of your heart. And you can make some of those decisions much easier when you *predetermine* your Best Yes event or activity. It's an intentional decision to underwhelm your schedule so you can overwhelm your soul. When a request comes your way that conflicts with your Best Yes, you can quickly and kindly turn it down.

In the group discussion, you had a chance to consider some of the desires you have but can't seem to make time for. Use the chart on the following page to write down two or three of the desires you identified. For each desire you write down, use the right column to brainstorm one or two ways you might predetermine a Best Yes on your calendar. (An example has been provided.)

Now briefly review your chart. As you consider the convictions of your heart—the ways in which you feel God might be leading you to move ahead—which one of the Best Yes ideas you wrote down do you feel most drawn to? Circle it on the chart. What hopes do you have for how this activity might give you joy or overwhelm your soul?

My Desires	Ideas for How I Might Predetermine a Best Yes
I want a welcoming home where my family can connect with each other and invest in relationships with people we care about.	*We can set aside Monday nights as family dinner and discussion nights. The kids can invite friends over and I'll trust that God will multiply any food we have!*

Now use this chart to identify any logistics you might need to consider in order to predetermine your Best Yes.

Logistics to Consider	To Predetermine My Best Yes, I Need to . . .
When do you want to schedule your Best Yes on your calendar? For example: Monday nights, the first Friday of the month, Saturday mornings, etc.	
What existing commitments might need to be rescheduled or declined?	
Whom do you need to coordinate with or get buy-in from? For example: a spouse, kids, etc.	
What other logistical or relational concerns might you need to address?	

"Commit everything you do to the LORD," wrote the psalmist. "Trust him, and he will help you" (Psalm 37:5 NLT). Take a moment to talk to God about your Best Yes desires and any next steps you've identified. Commit your plans to Him. Ask the Lord for the help you need to protect this Best Yes on your calendar.

Session 4

Personal Study

TEN TIMES WISE

Briefly identify a situation for which you need wisdom to discern a Best Yes in the near future.

Read through the ten verses from Proverbs on the following page. Check the box next to any verse that might relate to your issue. Now consider how the verse or verses you checked might apply to your situation and write down any connections you recognize.

Make the verse or verses you checked the focus of your prayer. Ask God to help you apply this wisdom as you seek to make a Best Yes choice.

TEN PROVERBS

- ❏ Friends love through all kinds of weather, and families stick together in all kinds of trouble (Proverbs 17:17 MSG).

- ❏ A sensible person accepts correction, but you can't beat sense into a fool (Proverbs 17:10 CEV).

- ❏ Enthusiasm without knowledge is no good; haste makes mistakes (Proverbs 19:2 NLT).

- ❏ It is to one's honor to avoid strife, and every fool is quick to quarrel (Proverbs 20:3 NIV).

- ❏ Don't say, "I will get even for this wrong." Wait for the Lord to handle the matter (Proverbs 20:22 NLT).

- ❏ When pride comes, then comes disgrace, but with humility comes wisdom (Proverbs 11:2 NIV).

- ❏ Clean living before God and justice with our neighbors mean far more to God than religious performance (Proverbs 21:3 MSG).

- ❏ A gossip will reveal your secrets! So avoid the company of people who talk openly and foolishly (Proverbs 20:19 The Voice).

- ❏ Mixed motives twist life into tangles; pure motives take you straight down the road (Proverbs 21:8 MSG).

- ❏ Do not let your heart envy sinners, but be zealous for the fear of the Lord all the day (Proverbs 23:17 NKJV).

Avoid the Traps of People Pleasing

If pleasing people were my goal,
I would not be Christ's servant.
Galatians 1:10 NLT

Recommended reading prior to the meeting:
The Best Yes book, chapters 13 – 15

GROUP DISCUSSION:
Checking In (5 minutes)

If your group meets for two hours, allow 15 minutes
for this discussion.

A key part of getting to know God better is sharing your journey with others. Before watching the video, briefly check in with each other about your experiences since the last session. For example:

- What insights did you discover in the personal study, reading through Proverbs, or in the chapters you read from *The Best Yes* book?
- How did the last session impact your daily life or your relationship with God?
- What questions would you like to ask the other members of your group?

VIDEO:
Avoid the Traps of People Pleasing (16 minutes)

Play the video segment for Session 5. As you watch, use the outline provided to follow along or to take additional notes on anything that stands out to you.

Notes

Sometimes I confuse the command to love with the disease to please: I dread saying yes but feel powerless to say no.

I get tripped up when I let my desire to please people outweigh my desire to please God.

It's not fun to be caught between two worlds — people pleasing and God pleasing.

"Fear of man will prove to be a snare, but whoever trusts in the Lord is kept safe" (Proverbs 29:25 NIV).

The Hebrew word for "fear" is *charadah* (khar-aw-daw´), which means trembling, quaking, to have an anxious care.

The Hebrew word for "snare" is *moqesh* (mo-kashe´), which means bait or lure.

The term "kept safe" is written as "exalted" in the New American Standard Bible. The Hebrew word is *sagab* (saw-gab´), which means inaccessibly high, too high for capture.

Having an anxious care about trying to win the approval of others can really get us into trouble. It can be a snare that lures us away from trusting God and following His best wisdom and plans for us.

When we decide to be more concerned with pleasing God than pleasing man, our trust in God elevates us and keeps us from getting caught in the trap of people pleasing.

The four traps of people pleasing (two fears and two needs):

+ The fear of rejection
+ The fear of disappointing people
+ The need to manage perceptions
+ The need for approval

"Many even among the leaders believed in him. But because of the Pharisees they would not confess their faith for fear they would be put out of the synagogue; for they loved praise from men more than praise from God" (John 12:42 – 43 NIV 1984).

We have to make the choice to trust God. That's the only thing that will elevate us past the snare of people pleasing.

We have to be careful with our desires.

"Am I now trying to win the approval of men, or of God? Or am I trying to please men? If I were still trying to please men, I would not be a servant of Christ" (Galatians 1:10 NIV 1984).

People pleasing is a trap. I have to make a choice between pleasing God and pleasing people.

How do we trust God? We acknowledge Him in all our ways.

"Trust God from the bottom of your heart; don't try to figure out everything on your own. Listen for God's voice in everything you do, everywhere you go; he's the one who will keep you on track. Don't assume that you know it all. Run to God! Run from evil!" (Proverbs 3:5 – 7 MSG).

This Week: Practice trusting God by continuing to utilize the power of the small no.

My Thoughts:

GROUP DISCUSSION:
Video Debrief (5 minutes)

> If your group meets for two hours, allow 10 minutes
> for this discussion.

1. What part of the teaching had the most impact on you?

The Disease to Please (8 minutes)

> If your group meets for two hours, allow 15 minutes
> for this discussion.

2. When you dread saying yes but feel powerless to say no, which of the following statements (see next page) comes closest to describing your thoughts? Choose one or two, and share the reasons for your response.

- ❑ I'd rather say yes than have a confrontation.
- ❑ I don't want people to think I'm selfish.
- ❑ I don't want this person to be mad at me.
- ❑ I want to be recognized as a person who can handle whatever comes my way.
- ❑ If I say yes, this person will like me, accept me, approve of me, etc.
- ❑ I want to be a nice person, and nice people don't say no.
- ❑ I'd rather overextend myself than disappoint someone whose opinion matters to me.
- ❑ If I say yes, this person is more likely to be there for me in the future when I want or need something.
- ❑ I want to be loving, and saying no does not seem loving.
- ❑ Other:

  _____

  _____

The Traps of People Pleasing (11 minutes)

If your group meets for two hours, allow 20 minutes for this discussion.

3. Lysa identified four prevalent traps of people pleasing: (1) the fear of rejection; (2) the fear of disappointing people; (3) the need to manage perceptions; and (4) the need for approval.

   ◆ Which of the four traps comes closest to describing the statement you chose in question 2?

+ In what areas of life are you most likely to fall into this trap? For example: at work, at church, on social media, while shopping, at home, at social gatherings, etc.

4. Switch perspectives for a moment and consider what it's like to be on the receiving end of people pleasing behaviors.

   + How do you tend to respond when someone engages in people pleasing behaviors toward you? For example: you sense that they are afraid of disappointing you, or they need your approval.

   + Are people pleasing behaviors in others more likely to put you at ease or to make you uncomfortable? Share any examples you can think of to illustrate your response.

   + In your experience, what distinguishes genuine helpfulness or a servant heart from people pleasing?

People Pleaser or God Pleaser? (13 minutes)

If your group meets for two hours, allow 16 minutes for this discussion.

5. Jesus understood the dangers of this people pleasing tendency in the human heart, and he warned His followers against it:

> "Be careful not to practice your righteousness in front of others to be seen by them. If you do, you will have no reward from your Father in heaven."
>
> (Matthew 6:1)

The behavior Jesus goes on to challenge is hypocrisy — specifically, making a public display of helping the poor in order to be honored and thought well of by others (Matthew 6:2). The Greek word used to describe "hypocrites" in Jesus' statement has its roots in the world of ancient Greek theater. A *hypokritēs* (hoop-ok-ree-tace′) was one who wore a mask and played a role — an actor. Over time, it came to mean someone who had "a double heart and false lips."[7] We get this sense of Jesus' statement in *The Message*:

> "Be especially careful when you are trying to be good so that you don't make a performance out of it. It might be good theater, but the God who made you won't be applauding."
>
> (Matthew 6:1 MSG)

+ What comes to mind when you think about people pleasing not so much as a loving thing to do but as a kind of theatrical performance?

+ In your own people pleasing, how would you describe the roles you tend to play? For example: the nice neighbor, the good daughter, the responsible employee, the sacrificial friend.

---

7 W. Günther, *"hypokritēs," New International Dictionary of New Testament Theology*, Colin Brown, gen. ed. (Grand Rapids: Zondervan, 1976, 1986), 468.

❧ In this role, how do you want your "audience" to respond? What do you most hope they will applaud in you?

❧ Making choices to please God alone is sometimes referred to as living for an audience of One. Why do you think it's so hard for most of us to shift our desire for acceptance and approval from people to God?

6. Author and pastor Dallas Willard acknowledges the spiritual impact when we make it a habit to seek approval from people rather than God:

> When we want human approval and esteem, and do what we do for the sake of it, God courteously stands aside because, by our wish, it does not concern him.... When our aim is to impress human beings ... he lets us do that.... On the other hand, if we live unto God alone, he responds to our expectations — which are of him alone.[8]

❧ The biblical wisdom is, "Fearing people is a dangerous trap, but trusting the LORD means safety" (Proverbs 29:25 NLT). Based on Willard's statement, how would you describe the trap of people pleasing, and the safety of trusting the Lord?

❧ Many people pleasing behaviors are misguided attempts to address some kind of legitimate unmet need — for recognition, approval, love, etc. How does it impact you to think that you

---

8 Dallas Willard, *The Divine Conspiracy* (New York: HarperCollins, 1998), 190.

might essentially be asking God to stand aside while you seek to meet your own needs?

OPTIONAL DISCUSSION:
BECOMING A BEST YES GROUP (17 MINUTES)

If your group meets for two hours, use this discussion as part of your meeting.

⁓

- What personal need are you trying to fulfill by choosing people pleasing? Some examples might be: acceptance, love, the desire to be noticed, etc.

- Where do you think this need originates?

- Write each person's name and contact information on a note card. Choose prayer partners again this session and use these cards to keep in touch. Be sure to pray that God will help your prayer partner with any people pleasing tendencies she might have. Remember to keep in touch throughout the week via phone, text, or email.

INDIVIDUAL ACTIVITY:
What I Want to Remember (2 minutes)

Complete this activity on your own.

1. Briefly review the outline and any notes you took.
2. In the space below, write down the most significant thing you gained in this session — from the teaching, activities, or discussions.

What I want to remember from this session ...

CLOSING PRAYER

Close your time together with prayer. Ask God to make you aware of those times when you tend toward people pleasing, and to help you shift your desire for acceptance and approval to Him alone.

GO DEEPER WITH *THE BEST YES*

For additional teaching and insights, read the following chapters in *The Best Yes* book if you haven't already done so:

13. But What If I Say No and They Stop Liking Me?
14. A Best Yes Is Seen by Those Who Choose to See
15. The Thrill of an Unrushed Yes

GET A HEAD START ON THE DISCUSSION FOR SESSION 6

As part of the group discussion for Session 6, you'll have an opportunity to talk about what you've learned and experienced together throughout *The Best Yes* study. Between now and your next meeting, consider taking a few moments to review the previous sessions and identify the teaching, discussions, or insights that stand out most to you. Use the worksheet on the following pages to briefly summarize the highlights of what you've learned and experienced.

Session 6

Head Start Worksheet

Take a few moments to reflect on what you've learned and experienced throughout *The Best Yes* study. You may want to review notes from the video teaching, what you wrote down for "What I Want to Remember" at the end of each group session, responses in the personal studies, etc. Here are some questions you might consider as part of your review:

- What insights did I gain from this session?
- What was the most important thing I learned about myself in this session?
- How did I experience God's presence or leading related to this session?
- How did this session impact my relationships with the other people in the group?

Use the spaces provided below and on the next page to briefly summarize what you've learned and experienced for each session.

Session 1:

SET YOUR HEART TO WISDOM

Session 2:
ESTABLISH A PATTERN OF WISDOM

Session 3:
PRACTICE WISDOM

Session 4:
PREDETERMINE YOUR BEST YES

Session 5:
AVOID THE TRAPS OF PEOPLE PLEASING

Wise Up

WEEK 5 READING WORKSHEET

If you're participating in the optional group challenge to read through the book of Proverbs, use this worksheet to help you keep track of your reading. If you'd like, use the space below to make notes and to reflect on what you read this week.

- ❑ Proverbs 26
- ❑ Proverbs 27
- ❑ Proverbs 28
- ❑ Proverbs 29
- ❑ Proverbs 30
- ❑ Proverbs 31

What verses, words, or phrases stand out most to you? Why?

When I alter
my Best Yes decisions
because I'm too afraid
to disappoint someone,
it just wears me out.
Saying yes all the time
won't make me
Wonder Woman.
It will make me a
worn-out woman.

Session 5

Personal Study

SEEING OPPORTUNITIES, SAYING YES

We can't just say yes because there's a project to be done. We have to say a Best Yes to the presence only we can offer. Be present in your life, right where you are, and dare to look. Look for the little everyday answers to decisions you have to make by being fully present.

The Best Yes, page 172

1. Not all Best Yes decisions are predetermined or require saying yes or no to someone's request. In fact, many times a Best Yes decision flows out of simply being present and saying yes to God in an ordinary moment. To get an idea of what this looks like in everyday life, read the personal story Lysa shares in "Pay Attention to What's in Front of You."

PAY ATTENTION TO WHAT'S IN FRONT OF YOU

The other day I was in a drive-thru early in the morning. . . . I wanted to surprise my daughter with one of her favorite biscuits. This eating establishment makes them every morning — golden brown on the top and bottom, fluffy in the middle, and good and buttered all around.

It's the kind of thing one can enjoy in the teen years. I'm at the age where I must avoid said items. It's sad but true.

What's also sad but true is the reason I had to get her biscuit at the drive-thru restaurant instead of just making biscuits at home. The ones I sometimes bake from popped-open cans shame the country cooking roots from which my people come. The women in my lineage handled a rolling pin as if it were a third arm. I don't even own a rolling pin. I don't think.

So my girl would be absolutely thrilled at this restaurant-bought, real biscuit.

I ordered it and grabbed my wallet for the necessary two dollars.

Two dollars isn't a big deal until you need it and don't have it. I scrambled through my purse, then the middle console of my car, and then in all the places change might have fallen. Nothing. I then decided I'd just use a credit card. Which would have been an amazing plan if only my credit card had been where it was supposed to be in my wallet.

That's when I got completely desperate and started praying for the person in front of me to please feel some sort of divine nudge to pay for my order. Maybe? Please?

But at the very last minute there was no need for that nudge. As I pulled up to the window I found my credit card wrapped up in a receipt at the bottom of my purse. Biscuit saved.

As I handed my credit card through the window I had the strangest notion to use that desperate feeling in an act of obedience. *Don't waste it. Let it make you aware. Be an extension of God's love right now.*

So I paid for the breakfast of the guy behind me. That's nothing new, right? But don't miss the point here. I don't want to focus on the act of paying for food. It's the revelation of paying attention.

Paying attention to what's in front of us will help us see our Best Yes. I saw what it felt like to need someone to pay for my breakfast, so I used it as a Best Yes. Not that every responsibility is our responsibility. . . . I mean, I didn't walk into the restaurant and buy everyone's breakfast. I just simply and quietly gave to the guy behind me.

I think this is the way Best Yes things often unfold. We want big directional signs from God. God just wants us to pay attention.

The Best Yes, pages 168 – 170

By being fully present — to herself, to what was happening, and to God — Lysa was able to transition a desperate feeling into a Best Yes. We can't plan for spontaneous decisions, but we can practice paying attention and get better at recognizing Best Yes opportunities when they come. One way to do this is to look back on the day before and search for any hidden treasures — opportunities we may have had to say a Best Yes but missed because we weren't paying attention to what was in front of us.

Use the chart on the following page to think back over the last twenty-four hours — morning, afternoon, and evening. For each time throughout the day, identify one hidden treasure. Consider especially inconveniences, interruptions, or anything that messed with your routine or your plans. Note what kept you from paying attention to the experience as a potential Best Yes opportunity. Then do a little brainstorming on how you might transition a similar opportunity into a Best Yes next time. (Lysa's story has been provided as an example.)

Yesterday's Hidden Treasures	How I Might Transition This to a Best Yes Next Time
Morning *There was a brief moment in the drive-thru when I thought I didn't have money to pay for the biscuit I'd just ordered.* **What Kept Me from Paying Attention** *I was in a hurry. And I was also caught up in how embarrassing it would be to have to tell the cashier that I didn't have the money to pay for my order!*	*After finding my credit card, I could extend God's love by buying breakfast for the guy behind me in the drive-thru.*
Morning **What Kept Me from Paying Attention**	
Afternoon **What Kept Me from Paying Attention**	
Evening **What Kept Me from Paying Attention**	

Briefly review the responses on your chart. What stands out to you about the kinds of things that kept you from paying attention and being fully present?

2. When we are fully present we focus our awareness on the here and now. But that can be hard to do when we feel rushed or overwhelmed. Author and pastor John Ortberg describes hurry as one of the greatest threats to our ability to be present:

> Being hurried is an inner condition, a condition of the soul. It means to be so preoccupied with myself and my life that I am unable to be fully present with God, with myself, and with other people. I am unable to occupy this present moment.... I cannot live in the kingdom of God with a hurried soul.[9]

To what degree was hurry a factor in the situations you listed on your chart? How did it keep you from being fully present to God, to yourself, and to other people?

3. We will see our Best Yes answers most clearly when we are present, paying attention, seeing what we need to see, and willing to extend God's love in the moment. We have a beautiful picture of how Jesus did this when He healed a suffering woman. Read the story, including some background, in Mark 5:21 – 34, and then respond to the questions on the next page.

---

9 John Ortberg, *Soul Keeping: Caring for the Most Important Part of You* (Grand Rapids: Zondervan, 2014), 130.

What circumstances might reasonably have caused Jesus to be hurried and kept Him from being fully present to the woman?

How specifically did Jesus remain present, pay attention, see what He needed to see, and extend God's love in the moment?

The first thing Jesus did after the woman touched Him was to stop what He was doing; even with a life-and-death situation on His agenda, He allowed Himself to be interrupted by the situation right in front of Him. The pressure of the crowd and the items on His to-do list didn't keep Him from attending to God's assignment for Him in the moment.

Overall, how would you describe your willingness to be interrupted? What is your typical reaction when you encounter an inconvenience or something that messes with your agenda or routine?

If you think of interruptions and inconveniences as God's invitations to stop what you're doing and pay attention, what divine invitations do you see hidden in the situations you listed on your chart?

A soul well spent will be one who lives Best Yes answers.... Are you ready now to dare to look at and extend God's love to what's right there and give it your Best Yes?

The Best Yes, page 178

4. Read Proverbs 4:25 – 26, which includes an encouragement to "look straight ahead, and fix your eyes on what lies before you" (NLT). Use the passage as a reference for writing your own prayer. Ask God to give you a heart that's willing to be interrupted. Seek His guidance to help you stop, pay attention, see what you need to see, and respond in love. Thank Him in advance for the divine invitations He will bring your way.

Session 5

Personal Study

YOU CAN'T PLEASE EVERYONE

Healthy relationships aren't void of service. Of course we must serve, love, give, be available, help, and contribute to the greater good. But we must have the freedom to say yes or no responsibly without fear of emotional consequences. To better understand what emotional consequences look like, read the personal story Lysa shares in "Fully Committed."

FULLY COMMITTED

I once volunteered with a woman who was constantly saying, "You know, God is looking for willing women." She would spiritually rationalize that if there are tasks in front of us, we should see them as our assignments. I was so afraid of telling her no. I felt like by doing so I was admitting spiritual weakness and huge deficiencies in my relationship with God.

A couple of times I tried to say no because I had small children, thus making it unrealistic for me to keep the same hours she did. I could tell she wasn't happy. When I asked her about it, she quickly remarked, "I'm so tired of hearing you say that

---

you have small children. We all know you have small children. Don't state the obvious. Just figure out how to make your
schedule work."

She wasn't trying to be mean. She wasn't trying to attack
me. She was honestly just trying to get a job done based on her
deep-down belief that propelled her to think Christian women
should please God by absolutely always saying yes to others'
requests.

That was a foundational belief in her life. But it was a faulty
foundational belief....

There is a verse that might add some clarity to this discussion: "For the eyes of the Lord range throughout the earth to
strengthen those whose hearts are fully committed to him"
(2 Chronicles 16:9). Great verse. But taken out of context, we
might develop the faulty belief that this is proof the Lord is
looking for people who will say yes to everything in front of
them. After all, isn't that what "fully committed" means?

No. There is a big difference between saying yes to everyone and saying yes to God.

The Best Yes, pages 162 – 163

A consequence is a penalty, something we suffer because of a
choice. An emotional consequence is a psychological penalty — and in
the context of relationships, it sometimes carries with it an undercur-
rent of intimidation. What emotional consequences do you recognize
in Lysa's story?

What aspects of her story do you relate to? For example, are there relationships or situations in which you anticipate emotional consequences if you were to say no or make an alternative choice?

Is this a behavior you recognize in yourself? In what ways, if any, do you sometimes create emotional consequences when someone says no to you?

Whenever we find ourselves saying yes when we need to say no, it's important to consider our motives. There is almost always a need we're trying to meet with people pleasing, and we discover it tucked into our thoughts about those decisions. For example: *If I do this, they will ... like me, do something for me, owe me a favor.* We answer the request by making a secret request and presuming we'll get it in return for our yes.

What secret requests have motivated some of your yes decisions?

In order to say a Best Yes, we need to be able to say yes without presuming this yes will be a way to feel more, have more, or have more owed to us. And we need to be able to say no without presuming this no will make us feel less, have less, or be owed less. Then we can say with the apostle Paul, "Our purpose is to please God, not people. He alone examines the motives of our hearts" (1 Thessalonians 2:4 NLT).

Take a moment to pray through the secret requests you identified. Invite God to be the one who meets those needs for you. Seek His guidance and wisdom for the decisions you face. Ask Him to give you the desire and power to do what pleases Him.

Session 5

Personal Study

TEN TIMES WISE

Briefly identify a situation for which you need wisdom to discern a Best Yes in the near future.

Read through the ten verses from Proverbs on the following page. Check the box next to any verse that might relate to your issue. Now consider how the verse or verses you checked might apply to your situation and write down any connections you recognize.

Make the verse or verses you checked the focus of your prayer. Ask God to help you apply this wisdom as you seek to make a Best Yes choice.

TEN PROVERBS

❑ There is no wisdom, no insight, no plan that can succeed against the LORD (Proverbs 21:30 NIV).

❑ Don't befriend angry people or associate with hot-tempered people, or you will learn to be like them and endanger your soul (Proverbs 22:24 – 25 NLT).

❑ Do not wear yourself out to get rich; do not trust your own cleverness (Proverbs 23:4 NIV).

❑ Patient persistence pierces through indifference; gentle speech breaks down rigid defenses (Proverbs 25:15 MSG).

❑ Better a dry crust with peace and quiet than a house full of feasting, with strife (Proverbs 17:1 NIV).

❑ Let someone else praise you, and not your own mouth; an outsider, and not your own lips (Proverbs 27:2 NIV).

❑ People ruin their lives by their own foolishness and then are angry at the LORD (Proverbs 19:3 NLT).

❑ Don't rejoice when your enemies fall; don't be happy when they stumble. For the LORD will be displeased with you (Proverbs 24:17 – 18 NLT).

❑ Wounds from a sincere friend are better than many kisses from an enemy (Proverbs 27:6 NLT).

❑ The name of the LORD is a fortified tower; the righteous run to it and are safe (Proverbs 18:10 NIV).

Build a Best Yes Legacy

I pray that your hearts will be flooded with light
so that you can understand the confident hope he has given
to those he called — his holy people who are his rich
and glorious inheritance.
Ephesians 1:18 NLT

Recommended reading prior to the meeting:
The Best Yes book, chapters 16 – 19

GROUP DISCUSSION:
Checking In (5 minutes)

If your group meets for two hours, allow 15 minutes
for this discussion.

A key part of getting to know God better is sharing your journey with others. Before watching the video, briefly check in with each other about your experiences since the last session. For example:

- What insights did you discover in the personal study, reading through Proverbs, or in the chapters you read from *The Best Yes* book?
- How did the last session impact your daily life or your relationship with God?
- What questions would you like to ask the other members of your group?

VIDEO:
Build a Best Yes Legacy (12 minutes)

Play the video segment for Session 6. As you watch, use the outline provided to follow along or to take additional notes on anything that stands out to you.

Notes

Legacies of a Best Yes life lived out in Scripture include:

- Moses, the most humble man on earth
- David, a man after God's own heart
- Solomon, the wisest man who ever lived
- Noah, righteous before God
- Peter, the rock
- Mary, the mother of Jesus, highly favored

Each one made daily choices — small and large — to weave the threads of their Best Yes answers into a legacy.

Legacies are the generous, selfless, quiet choices that honor God in the midst of a day. Legacies are daily.

It's easy to be intimidated or discouraged by the legacies of these people. But the Bible also highlights their failures and frailties:

- Moses didn't always follow God's instructions and paid a steep price.
- David committed adultery.
- Solomon had 700 wives and 300 concubines that led him to worship other gods.
- Noah had a situation with drunkenness and nakedness.
- Peter denied Jesus.
- Mary overstepped.

They had momentary lapses, but their Best Yes decisions were so deeply woven into the fabric of their lives that their failures didn't destroy their legacies.

C. S. Lewis made a simple decision to handwrite a reply to every letter he received. This practice of letter writing was a Best Yes for him.

Your Best Yes doesn't have to be a big event or grand accomplishment; it can be a simple, daily decision. Pause in the midst of the daily rush to show up and build your legacy.

Making wise decisions in the midst of trying times can lead to a much bigger Best Yes around the corner — a yes that will become part of your legacy.

The choices I make today will build a legacy for this twenty-four hours. I make my choices and then my choices make me.

"That's why, when I heard of the solid trust you have in the Master Jesus and your outpouring of love to all the followers of Jesus, I couldn't stop thanking God for you — every time I prayed, I'd think of you and give thanks. But I do more than thank. I ask — ask the God of our Master, Jesus Christ, the God of glory — to make you intelligent and discerning in knowing him personally, your eyes focused and clear, so that you can see exactly what it is he is calling you to do, grasp the immensity of this glorious way of life he has for his followers, oh, the utter extravagance of his work in us who trust him — endless energy, boundless strength!" (Ephesians 1:15 – 19 MSG).

This Week: Identify a word or phrase that you would like to be part of your lifelong legacy. For example: *loving, strong, patient, kind*. Then make a small and simple choice to live out that word or phrase in the course of an ordinary day — a twenty-four-hour legacy.

My Thoughts:

GROUP DISCUSSION:
Video Debrief (5 minutes)

If your group meets for two hours, allow 15 minutes
for this discussion.

1. What part of the teaching had the most impact on you?

Decision Making Confidence (7 minutes)

If your group meets for two hours, allow 9 minutes
for this discussion.

2. At the beginning of the video, Lysa invited you to imagine what
   it could be like to feel fully confident in the decisions you make.
   Overall, how would you describe your level of decision-making
   confidence right now? Circle the number on the continuum that
   best describes your response.

1   2   3   4   5   6   7   8   9   10

Low Confidence   **High Confidence**
I have little to no   I have great
confidence in my   confidence in my
decision making.   decision making.

How do you feel about the number you circled? Would you say it's most representative of your *growth* in confidence, or of your *need for growth* in confidence? Share the reasons for your response.

Daily Legacy Choices (12 minutes)

> If your group meets for two hours, allow 23 minutes for this discussion.

3. We tend to think of a legacy as something big, and in one way it is — it is the impact of a lifetime. But Lysa also described a legacy as something we *build* over a lifetime — an accumulation of generous, selfless, quiet choices that honor God in the midst of a day.

   ✦ Who has left (or is leaving) this kind of legacy to you personally?

   ✦ Which of their quiet, daily choices stand out most to you? Why?

   ✦ Lysa pointed out that several of the biblical characters who left great legacies also had great failures, but their failures didn't destroy their legacies. Would you say the same about the person(s) you named? What role do their failures or weaknesses play in how you view them and their legacy?

♦ Which of their insights, lessons, or encouragements are most
meaningful to you as you consider building your own legacy?

4. One way to begin thinking about a lifetime legacy is to start with
a one-day legacy, what Lysa described as a twenty-four-hour gift.
As a way to get started in thinking about what a one-day legacy
might look like, consider the nine fruits of the Spirit described by
the apostle Paul (Galatians 5:22 – 23).

Love	Patience	Faithfulness
Joy	Kindness	Gentleness
Peace	Goodness	Self-control

♦ Think back over the last day or two and identify a "legacy" left
by someone else. What quiet choice, small decision, or selfless
action did he or she make? Which fruit of the Spirit comes closest to describing that legacy?

♦ Imagine that you were guaranteed to leave a legacy in the next
twenty-four hours. In addition to the foundation of love, which
fruit of the Spirit represents the legacy you would most like to
leave? What impact would you hope it might have — on you as
well as on others?

The Legacy of Best Yes Choices (9 minutes)

> If your group meets for two hours, allow 15 minutes
> for this discussion.

5. We tend to think that our weaknesses detract from our legacy, but how we handle our frail places and disappointments can become the very thing that makes our legacy shine brightest.

   Imagine for a moment that you are on the other side of the disappointments or weaknesses you're struggling with now. How would you describe the legacy you want your decisions to leave during this trying time?

6. Best Yes choices don't have to be big events or grand accomplishments. Mother Teresa once said, "Don't look for big things, just do small things with great love … the smaller the thing, the greater must be our love."[10]

   ✦ What examples or personal experiences can you think of that demonstrate what it means to do small things with great love?

   ✦ The second half of Mother Teresa's statement suggests that the small choices we make potentially require more of us than the big choices, because they must be done with greater love. Do you find this idea challenging or encouraging? Share the reasons for your response.

---

10 Mother Teresa, *Come Be My Light*, Brian Kolodiejchuk, M.C., ed. (New York: Doubleday, 2007), 34.

The Purpose of Wisdom (8 minutes)

If your group meets for two hours, allow 15 minutes
for this discussion.

7. At the end of the video, Lysa shared these words from the apostle
Paul, who prayed them for the church at Ephesus:

> I keep asking that the God of our Lord Jesus Christ, the glorious Father, may give you the Spirit of wisdom and revelation, so that you may know him better. I pray that the eyes of your heart may be enlightened in order that you may know the hope to which he has called you, the riches of his glorious inheritance in his holy people, and his incomparably great power for us who believe.
>
> (Ephesians 1:17 – 19 NIV)

Paul links the purpose of wisdom directly to our relationship with Christ. How might it change the way you approach your decisions if the first question you asked was not, "How can I choose what's best in this situation?" but, "How can I choose Christ in this situation and get to know Him better?"

OPTIONAL DISCUSSION:
BECOMING A BEST YES GROUP (18 MINUTES)

If your group meets for two hours, use this discussion
as part of your meeting.

ᢍ

Take a few moments to discuss what you've learned and experienced together throughout *The Best Yes* study.

- What would you say is the most important thing you learned or experienced? How has it impacted you? For example: in your attitudes, behaviors, relationships, etc.

- How have you recognized God at work in your life through the study?

- How might you continue to pray for one another moving forward?

INDIVIDUAL ACTIVITY:
What I Want to Remember (2 minutes)

Complete this activity on your own.

1. Briefly review the outline and any notes you took.
2. In the space below, write down the most significant thing you gained in this session — from the teaching, activities, or discussions.

What I want to remember from this session ...

CLOSING PRAYER

Close your time together with prayer. Ask God for the strength and guidance you need to "choose Christ" in all things so that you might come to know Him better with every decision you make.

GO DEEPER WITH *THE BEST YES*

For additional teaching and insights, read the following chapters in *The Best Yes* book if you haven't already done so:

16. The Panic that Keeps You from Your Best Yes
17. The Very Best Yes
18. When My Best Yes Doesn't Yield What I Expect
19. We Make Choices. Then Our Choices Make Us.

Let's choose wisdom.

Let's use the two most

powerful words, yes and no,

with resounding assurance,

graceful clarity,

and guided power.

All so people may

see Jesus

when they see us.

Hear Jesus

when they hear us.

And know Jesus

when they know us.

Session 6

Personal Study

OVERCOMING INSECURITIES AND FEARS

> It takes courage to step into this Best Yes mindset. It takes courage to say no. It takes courage to say yes. It takes courage to change the unhealthy patterns of our decision making. And any time we need to be courageous, our deepest insecurities can make us want to back down from change.
>
> *The Best Yes*, pages 193 – 194

1. An insecurity is that inner feeling of unease when we see ourselves as vulnerable, inferior, or threatened in some way. For example:

   I'm not as talented or smart or experienced as her; therefore, this new project won't ever really take off.

   My kids just demonstrated every inadequacy I have as a mom.

   I have to protect my dignity and myself. I don't dare try this new venture.

   If only I were as organized or intentional or creative as they are, then maybe I could accomplish this. But the reality is, I'm not.

171

See what he just said about me? He knows me better than anyone, so if he thinks that's true, it must be.

This relationship won't ever get any better.

Use the chart below to identify a few ways in which you want to change your patterns of decision making or move ahead with a Best Yes but haven't yet done so. Then identify any insecurities that come to mind when you think about making changes or moving ahead.

Ways in Which I Want to Change My Patterns of Decision Making or Move Ahead with a Best Yes	Insecurities I Am Aware Of

> We don't have to just manage our insecurities, deal with our insecurities, or grit our teeth and will ourselves to somehow ignore them. We can grow past them.
>
> *The Best Yes*, page 197

2. There are two particular patterns of thought that can either feed our insecurities or help us grow past them: a fixed mindset versus a growth mindset.

   Fixed mindset: A person with a fixed mindset sees her abilities, talents, skills, relationships, and intelligence as limited and lacking. Where she is today is where she will always be. Things can't get better. It is what it is. She thinks, "Applying this Best Yes wisdom isn't really possible for a person like me."

   Growth mindset: A person with a growth mindset sees her abilities, talents, skills, relationships, and intelligence with potential. Where she is today is a starting place, not a finish line. Things can get better. She can grow and develop and persevere to get to improved places. She thinks, "Using wisdom to make Best Yes decisions is possible!"

   Stanford University psychologist Carol Dweck, who pioneered this mindset idea, writes:

   > In a fixed mindset, people believe their basic qualities, like their intelligence or talent, are simply fixed traits. They spend their time documenting their intelligence or talent instead of developing them. They also believe that talent alone creates success — without effort. They're wrong.
   >
   > In a growth mindset, people believe that their most basic abilities can be developed through dedication and hard work — brains and talent are just the starting point. This view creates a love of learning and a resilience that is essential for great accomplishment.[11]

---

11 Carol S. Dweck, "Mindset: What Is It?" mindsetonline.com

Listed below are six paired statements that contrast a fixed mindset with a growth mindset. Keeping in mind the insecurities you identified in question 1, mark an X on each continuum to indicate how you would describe your mindset is right now.

●————————————————————————————————●

I Am Limited
I see my intelligence, talents, and relationships as limited and lacking.

I Have Potential
I see my intelligence, talents, and relationships as having potential.

●————————————————————————————————●

I Am a Finish Line
It's very unlikely that things will get better. Where I am today is where I will likely always be.

I Am a Starting Place
Things can get better. I can grow, develop, and persevere to get to a better place.

●————————————————————————————————●

I Am Complacent
I settle for leaving my intelligence and talents where they are now.

I Am Developing
I actively and routinely look for ways to develop my intelligence and talents.

●————————————————————————————————●

It's Not Possible
I don't think it's possible to use wisdom to make Best Yes decisions.

It Is Possible
I believe it is possible for me to use wisdom to make Best Yes decisions.

●————————————————————————————————●

It's about Talent
I don't have the talent or abilities I need to succeed.

It's about Dedication
I can develop even my most basic abilities with dedication and hard work.

●————————————————————————————————●

Failure Is Unacceptable
I cannot overcome if I fail.

Failure Is Part of Learning
I can be resilient and grow through failure.

Based on your continuum responses, how would you characterize your overall mindset right now?

For any continuums on which you placed your mark closer to the left than the right, how would you describe the appeal or benefit of having a fixed mindset in that area? In other words, why might you be willing to settle for a fixed mindset rather than a growth mindset in that area?

> We find security when we tie our mindsets to the potential of Jesus' work in us. Indeed we are limited in and of ourselves. But the minute we receive Jesus to be the Lord of our lives, our limited potential can turn into exponential growth. He is alive in us. He gives us freedom from our dead lives and the power to walk in a new life — a resurrected life.
>
> *The Best Yes*, page 197

3. In Romans 8, the apostle Paul provides a beautiful description of what it means to walk in the power of a new life — the potential of Jesus' work in us. Keeping your insecurities and fears in mind, read slowly and prayerfully through the two versions of the passage that follow. Underline any words or phrases that stand out to you.

The Spirit of God, who raised Jesus from the dead, lives in you. And just as God raised Christ Jesus from the dead, he will give life to your mortal bodies by this same Spirit living within you.

Therefore, dear brothers and sisters, you have no obligation to do what your sinful nature urges you to do. For if you live by its dictates, you will die. But if through the power of the Spirit you put to death the deeds of your sinful nature, you will live. For all who are led by the Spirit of God are children of God.

So you have not received a spirit that makes you fearful slaves. Instead, you received God's Spirit when he adopted you as his own children. Now we call him, "Abba, Father."

(Romans 8:11 – 15 NLT)

When God lives and breathes in you (and he does, as surely as he did in Jesus), you are delivered from that dead life. With his Spirit living in you, your body will be as alive as Christ's!

So don't you see that we don't owe this old do-it-yourself life one red cent. There's nothing in it for us, nothing at all. The best thing to do is give it a decent burial and get on with your new life. God's Spirit beckons. There are things to do and places to go!

This resurrection life you received from God is not a timid, grave-tending life. It's adventurously expectant, greeting God with a childlike "What's next, Papa?"

(Romans 8:11 – 15 MSG)

What connections do you make between your insecurities and the words and phrases you underlined?

The passages contrast being fearful slaves (living "a timid, grave-tending life") with being children of God (living an "adventurously expectant" life). What needs to receive a "decent burial" in order for you to live more fully into your identity as a child of God?

In what ways do you sense God's Spirit beckoning you? What do you sense God's answer might be if you were to ask, "What's next, Papa?"

> We must let our identity, not our insecurity, be the first thing that walks into every situation we face — every decision we make.
>
> *The Best Yes*, page 202

4. Our identity is that we are children of God, but when we chain our insecurities to our identity, we'll end up in a fixed mindset:

   I am a child of God, **but** *look at what a mess my finances are.*

   I am a child of God, **but** *I'm fifty pounds overweight and feel like such a failure.*

   I am a child of God, **but** *look at the choice my kid just made that makes our family look bad.*

In a growth mindset, we chain our identity to the Word of God. Every time we say I am a child of God, we remove the *but* and use the word *therefore* to usher God's promise into our reality:

I am a child of God, **therefore** *I don't have to be afraid or dismayed. I know God is with me. He will strengthen me, help me, and uphold me with His hand* (Isaiah 41:10).

I am a child of God, **therefore** *no weapon formed against me shall succeed. God will disprove every tongue that rises against me in judgment* (Isaiah 54:17).

I am a child of God, **therefore** *God is in my midst, a mighty One who will save me; He will rejoice over me with gladness, He will quiet me with his love; He will exult over me with loud singing* (Zephaniah 3:17).

I am a child of God, **therefore** *God's Word is there for me. It is a lamp to my feet and a light to my path* (Psalm 119:105).

Briefly refer back to the insecurities you listed on your chart in question 1. Using the statements above as a reference, write a "therefore" statement for each of your insecurities.

Read Psalm 27, a psalm of confidence and trust in God. Use the psalm as a reference for writing your own prayer. Acknowledge your insecurities and the fears that keep you from moving forward and living in a growth mindset. Ask God to "beckon" you, giving you a desire to live more fully as His child and an eagerness to take your next best step. Thank Him for being your stronghold.

Session 6

Personal Study

PREPARE FOR THE UNEXPECTED

Sometimes, bad things just happen. No matter how well we plan or pray, no matter how hard we work, something completely unexpected knocks us off our feet. Thousands of years ago, the writer of Ecclesiastes described the ambush of the unexpected this way:

> I have seen something else under the sun: The race is not to the swift or the battle to the strong, nor does food come to the wise or wealth to the brilliant or favor to the learned; but time and chance happen to them all. Moreover, no one knows when their hour will come: As fish are caught in a cruel net, or birds are taken in a snare, so people are trapped by evil times that fall unexpectedly upon them.
>
> (Ecclesiastes 9:11 – 12 NIV)

On first take, that may not seem like especially good news, but it's at least encouraging to know that the Bible acknowledges this hard reality. And yet, as Lysa affirms in "When the Unexpected Barges In," sudden hardships also offer a unique opportunity.

WHEN THE UNEXPECTED BARGES IN

We make the best decision we know to make. We pray. We ask God to guide us. We walk with Him and talk with Him and trust Him. We read the Christian books and get the Christian advice. We hang with Christians and sing the praise songs and use words like *blessed*, *calling*, and *fellowship*. We gather around the potluck dinner and wonder why the worship leader looks cool in what on us would be ridiculous.

We do all that. And still.

The unexpected barges in and announces he's staying for a while. Like a cuss word yelled by a heckler in a church service, it catches us off guard, makes us squirm, and needs to be ushered out of the building. But it lingers. And people whisper about it. And we wonder if the pastor should keep on preaching or call it a day.

Cuss words aren't supposed to be heard in church. And good mamas aren't supposed to feel like failures.

And wives who have loved well aren't supposed to be told their husbands have had affairs or find their husbands are addicted to porn.

And men who have worked hard, stayed late, and given all their best to a boss who treats them crappy aren't supposed to be fired.

And adoptive parents aren't supposed to have to give the answer to a million prayers back to a biological mom who will get high this afternoon.

And professional women aren't supposed to be told they can't have the big accounts because they refuse to go to the strip clubs with seedy clients.

(cont.)

And cancellation notices aren't supposed to be sent from a would-be bride flushed red with rejection.

You know what I'm saying? Have you ever felt knocked off-kilter by the unexpected? . . .

Often when things don't add up, we throw a spotlight on our weaknesses, don't we?

This situation stinks because I stink as a person.

My child failed because I failed as a mother.

My ministry didn't take off like I expected it to because I'm not smart enough, or schooled enough, or business minded enough.

I try so hard. I give it all I've got. Then it all just falls apart. And it all just seems incredibly out of whack.

But don't you see, in the midst of the unexpected we have the opportunity to make one of our greatest Best Yes decisions ever. Let this unexpected happening point to your strength, not your weakness. Maybe you've been entrusted with this. Not cursed with it.

The Best Yes, pages 219 – 222

Use the cloud illustration on the next page to write your responses to the following questions.

- As you read Lysa's list of "aren't supposed to" examples, what unexpected hardship came to mind from your own life?
- If you were to allow this experience to point to your weakness, where would it lead you (mentally, emotionally, spiritually)? For example, "My child failed because I failed as a mother."
- If you allowed it to point to your strength instead, where would it lead you (mentally, emotionally, spiritually)? For example, "I can pray my child through this situation and rely on God to write my child's story."

My Unexpected Hardship

My Weakness   My Strength

In the short term, unexpected hardships make no sense. They hurt. They'll make you angry. But you can't let them paralyze you. No matter what wrong thing has happened, Scripture affirms there is always a right next thing to do.

> Those who are wise will find a time and a way to do what is right, for there is a time and a way for everything, even when a person is in trouble.
>
> (Ecclesiastes 8:5 – 6 NLT)

What is the next right thing that's right in front of you? How do you sense God may be inviting you to respond to your unexpected hardship?

Read James 1:4 – 5, which describes the rewards of perseverance and God's promise of generous wisdom. Ask God for the wisdom you need to take your next step, and then the step after that. Choice by choice, day by day, your Best Yes answers will come.

Session 6

Personal Study

TEN TIMES WISE

Briefly identify a situation for which you need wisdom to discern a Best Yes in the near future.

Read through the ten verses from Proverbs on the following page. Check the box next to any verse that might relate to your issue. Now consider how the verse or verses you checked might apply to your situation and write down any connections you recognize.

Make the verse or verses you checked the focus of your prayer. Ask God to help you apply this wisdom as you seek to make a Best Yes choice.

TEN PROVERBS

❑ People who conceal their sins will not prosper, but if they confess and turn from them, they will receive mercy (Proverbs 28:13 NLT).

❑ If you have good sense, you will listen and obey; if all you do is talk, you will destroy yourself (Proverbs 10:8 CEV).

❑ She speaks with wisdom, and faithful instruction is on her tongue (Proverbs 31:26 NIV).

❑ Whoever stubbornly refuses to accept criticism will be suddenly destroyed beyond recovery (Proverbs 29:1 NLT).

❑ Fearing people is a dangerous trap, but trusting the LORD means safety (Proverbs 29:25 NLT).

❑ Speak up for those who cannot speak for themselves, for the rights of all who are destitute. Speak up and judge fairly; defend the rights of the poor and needy (Proverbs 31:8 – 9 NIV).

❑ There is more hope for a fool than for someone who speaks without thinking (Proverbs 29:20 NLT).

❑ Honest correction is appreciated more than flattery (Proverbs 28:23 CEV).

❑ Mercy to the needy is a loan to God, and God pays back those loans in full (Proverbs 19:17 MSG).

❑ Whoever has no rule over his own spirit is like a city broken down, without walls (Proverbs 25:28 NKJV).

About the Author

LYSA TERKEURST IS A WIFE TO ART AND MOM TO FIVE priority blessings named Jackson, Mark, Hope, Ashley, and Brooke. She is the president of Proverbs 31 Ministries and author of seventeen books, including the *New York Times* bestsellers *Unglued* and *Made to Crave*. Additionally, Lysa has been featured on *Focus on the Family*, *The Today Show*, *Good Morning America*, and more. Lysa speaks nationwide at Catalyst, Women of Faith, and various church events.

To those who know her best, Lysa is simply a carpooling mom who loves Jesus passionately, is dedicated to her family, and struggles like the rest of us with laundry, junk drawers, and cellulite.

❧

WEBSITE: If you enjoyed *The Best Yes*, equip yourself with additional resources at www.TheBestYes.com, www.LysaTerKeurst.com, and www.Proverbs31.org.

SOCIAL MEDIA: Connect with Lysa on a daily basis, see pictures of her family, and follow her speaking schedule:

- BLOG: www.LysaTerKeurst.com
- FACEBOOK: www.Facebook.com/OfficialLysa
- INSTAGRAM: @LysaTerKeurst
- TWITTER: @LysaTerKeurst

ABOUT PROVERBS 31 MINISTRIES

Lysa TerKeurst is the president of Proverbs 31 Ministries, located in Charlotte, North Carolina.

If you were inspired by *The Best Yes* and desire to deepen your own personal relationship with Jesus Christ, we encourage you to connect with Proverbs 31 Ministries.

We exist to be a trusted friend who will take you by the hand and walk by your side, leading you one step closer to the heart of God through:

- Free online daily devotions
- Online Bible studies
- Daily radio programs
- Books and resources

For more information about Proverbs 31 Ministries, visit: www.Proverbs31.org.

To inquire about having Lysa speak at your event, visit www.LysaTerKeurst.com and click on "speaking."

The Best Yes

Making Wise Decisions in the Midst of Endless Demands

Lysa TerKeurst,
New York Times *Bestselling Author*

Overwhelmed schedule = Underwhelmed soul

There's a big difference between saying yes to everyone and saying yes to God.

Lysa TerKeurst knows how it feels to live with the stress of an overwhelmed schedule and ache with the sadness of an underwhelmed soul. In *The Best Yes* she will help you

- Cure the disease to please with a better understanding of the command to love.
- Escape the shame and guilt of disappointing others by learning the secret of the small no.
- Overcome the agony of hard choices by embracing a wisdom based decision-making process.
- Rise above the rush of endless demands and discover the power of your Best Yes today.

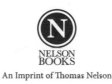

NELSON
BOOKS

An Imprint of Thomas Nelson

Unglued

Making Wise Choices in the Midst of Raw Emotions

Lysa TerKeurst
New York Times *Bestselling Author*

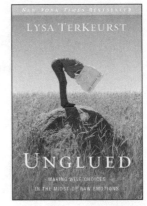

God gave us emotions to experience life, not destroy it! Lysa TerKeurst admits that she, like most women, has had experiences where others bump into her happy and she comes emotionally unglued. We stuff, we explode, or we react somewhere in between. What do we do with these raw emotions? Is it really possible to make emotions work for us instead of against us? Yes, and in her usual inspiring and practical way, Lysa will show you how. Filled with gut-honest personal examples and biblical teaching, *Unglued* will equip you to:

- Know with confidence how to resolve conflict in your important relationships.
- Find peace in your most difficult relationships as you learn to be honest but kind when offended.
- Identify what type of reactor you are and how to significantly improve your communication.
- Respond with no regrets by managing your tendencies to stuff or explode.
- Gain a deep sense of calm by responding to situations out of your control.

Also Available:

Unglued Curriculum

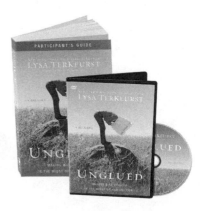

Made to Crave

Satisfying Your Deepest Desire with God, Not Food

Lysa TerKeurst,
New York Times *Bestselling Author*

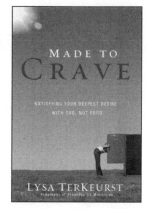

Made to Crave is the missing link between a woman's desire to be healthy and the spiritual empowerment necessary to make that happen. The reality is we were made to crave. Craving isn't a bad thing. But we must realize God created us to crave more of Him. Many of us have misplaced that craving by overindulging in physical pleasures instead of lasting spiritual satisfaction. If you are struggling with unhealthy eating habits, you can break the "I'll start again Monday" cycle, and start feeling good about yourself today. Learn to stop beating yourself up over the numbers on the scale. Discover that your weight loss struggle isn't a curse but rather a blessing in the making, and replace justifications that lead to diet failure with empowering go-to scripts that lead to victory. You can reach your healthy weight goal—and grow closer to God in the process.

Also Available:

Made to Crave Curriculum

Becoming More Than a Good Bible Study Girl

Lysa TerKeurst,
New York Times *Bestselling Author*

Is Something Missing in Your Life?

Lysa TerKeurst knows what it's like to consider God just another thing on her to-do list. For years she went through the motions of a Christian life: Go to church. Pray. Be nice.

Longing for a deeper connection between what she knew in her head and her everyday reality, she wanted to personally experience God's presence.

Drawing from her own remarkable story of step-by-step faith, Lysa invites you to uncover the spiritually exciting life we all yearn for. With her trademark wit and spiritual wisdom, Lysa will help you:

- Learn how to make a Bible passage come alive in your own devotion time.
- Replace doubt, regret, and envy with truth, confidence, and praise.
- Stop the unhealthy cycles of striving and truly learn to love who you are and what you've been given.
- Discover how to have inner peace and security in any situation.
- Sense God responding to your prayers.

The adventure God has in store for your life just might blow you away.

Also Available:

Becoming More Than a Good Bible Study Girl Curriculum

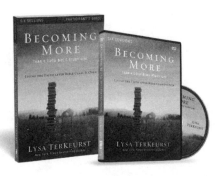